Deliberate Self-Harm in Adolescence

Child and Adolescent Mental Health Series

Written for professionals, and parents, these accessible, evidence-based resources are essential reading for anyone seeking to understand and promote children and young people's mental health. Drawing on the work of FOCUS, a multidisciplinary project based at the Royal College of Psychiatrists' Research Unit, each title in the series brings together practical and policy-level suggestions with up-to-the-minute analysis of research.

also in the series

Mental Health Services for Minority Ethnic Children and Adolescents
Edited by Mhemooda Malek and Carol Joughin
Foreword by Kedar Nath Dwivedi
ISBN 978 1 84310 236 6

Child and Adolescent Mental Health series

FOCUS

Deliberate Self-Harm in Adolescence

Claudine Fox and Keith Hawton

The Royal College of
Psychiatrists' Research Unit

Jessica Kingsley Publishers
London and Philadelphia

Contents

Acknowledgements

FOCUS is grateful to Carol Joughin and Professor Phillip Graham for providing advice and comments on drafts of this book.

The FOCUS Project is funded by a grant from the Gatsby Charitable Foundation and the Department of Health (Section 64 grant award).

Preface

Suicidal behaviour is increasingly found in young people. In fact, suicide is the third leading cause of death within this age group. Rates of attempted suicide are also usually found to be highest in people during the teenage years and twenties. It is not surprising therefore that suicide and attempted suicide as a field of research has grown in recent years. It is important for research to try and understand the causes and correlates of adolescent suicidal behaviour to enable more effective treatment interventions to be developed. Closer study of suicidal behaviour in young people will also aid in the identification of at-risk groups and better methods of prevention. In addition, it is important for research to address the stigma attached to suicidal behaviour in order to try to reduce the negative response that is generated. This in turn should facilitate discussion and the seeking of help and perhaps increase treatment compliance.

FOCUS is a child and adolescent mental health project that aims to promote effective, evidence-based practice in child and adolescent mental health services (CAMHS) through the dissemination of information. FOCUS produces evidence-based publications, which review the existing literature and critically appraise research in order to establish the quality of the research base with respect to different topic areas within CAMHS.

This book is written with this aim in mind, and as such begins by discussing general issues related to deliberate self-harm in adolescence, incorporating problems with definition and common myths associated with suicidal behaviour. It provides data on prevalence, discussing hospital data and data obtained from community-based samples. Chapter Three examines risk factors associated with suicidal behaviour utilizing critically appraised research papers in order to investigate whether there are links between depression, substance abuse and antisocial behaviour and suicidal behaviour. Chapter Four turns to screening instruments for the identification of at-risk individuals, incorporating critical appraisal of key instruments relevant to adolescents. Chapter Five provides practical information about commissioning and delivering services for young people who engage in deliberate self-harm. The management and prevention of suicidal behaviour are also tackled, incorporating critically appraised research to answer questions about the efficacy of aftercare and its outcome and the effectiveness of school-based suicide prevention programmes. The book concludes by discussing key messages and implications for the future. The Appendix contains information about the process involved in the identification of the literature and the critical appraisal of research papers relating to the issues of the efficacy of aftercare and its outcome, links of suicidal behaviour with psychiatric diagnoses and child to adult follow-up. It is hoped that this will provide some insight into what is involved in finding and evaluating the research in order to establish how good the evidence-base actually is.

The aim of the book is to provide a summary of information on deliberate self-harm in adolescence in order to highlight the current understanding and position of research within the field, with respect to a number of important issues. These include the efficacy of aftercare and its outcome, screening instruments for the identification of at-risk individuals, links of suicidal behaviour with psychiatric disorders and child to adult follow-up. It is hoped that the book will assist not only child and adolescent mental health professionals and any other professionals working with adolescents who engage in self-harming behaviour, but will also be of interest to parents and carers of children and adolescents who deliberately self-harm.

1 Introduction

Deliberate self-harm is a serious public health problem. A marked increase in the number of people engaging in attempted suicide has been observed since the mid-1960s. It is only within the last decade however that a growing volume of research on adolescent suicide and deliberate self-harm has emerged. In England and Wales alone there are 142,000 admissions to accident and emergency departments for deliberate self-harm each year. It is estimated that approximately 25,000 of those that present to accident and emergency departments are young people (Hawton *et al.* 2000).

Although the epidemiology of attempted suicide has been well documented within the United Kingdom, it is questionable how good the evidence-base is. Information on adolescent suicidal behaviour is obtained from a number of data sources, for example from those who compile data of deaths, usually based on the coroner's findings, or hospital records. Data obtained from sources such as these may not provide a true picture of the numbers of people who engage in self-harming behaviour however. That is, information obtained from hospital records reflects a documentation of the number of people that present to accident and emergency departments and the number of people that are discharged from inpatient care as a result of self-harming behaviour. Problems arise with using figures from sources such as these because there is inconsistency in the way that different hospitals collect and record data and more importantly, the majority of cases of deliberate self-harm do not come to the attention of the emergency services. This is because deliberate self-harm is often not an attempt at fatal injury, but an attempt to inflict harm without the need for medical attention.

A number of myths have arisen around the issue of suicidal behaviour. For example, that people who self-harm are looking for attention, that self-harm does not hurt or that how serious the problem is depends on the severity of the injury.

Deliberate self-harmers are 'attention seeking'

People who self-harm tend to do so in private, on parts of the body that are not visible to others. They often do not tell friends or family and due to stigma and low self-esteem are unlikely to seek help.

> Cutting myself is such a private thing. I find it hard to talk to other people about how I feel. They don't understand. They think I'm seeking attention – that's the last thing I want. (Spandler 1996, p.77)

Self-harming 'does not hurt'

Although the initial sensation may be blunted due to the intensity of emotion, self-harming does hurt. In fact, it is common for the sense of pain to be amplified by the time the person is receiving treatment. Each person will have a different pain threshold however.

The seriousness of the problem can be measured by the severity of injury

This is not the case. A person who hurts themselves a bit can be feeling just as bad as someone who hurts themselves a lot.

It is perhaps not surprising that the reality is very different from the impression given by the common myths described above. The following case example may help to highlight this point.

> Rachel, aged 16 years, had presented many times to the general hospital with self-harm behaviour, usually involving wrist cutting and/or overdose with over-the-counter analgesic medication. The precipitant was most often conflict with her adoptive mother, who was at a loss to know how to manage her. Rachel met diagnostic criteria for borderline personality disorder, complicated by sub-

stance misuse and dysthymia. She had not attended school for two years. Once in hospital Rachel would often cut herself again using a razor blade hidden in her belongings. Recognizing that there was a pattern to Rachel's behaviour, the consultant psychiatrist providing outpatient treatment organized for Rachel to always be admitted to the same medical ward, where a very experienced nursing sister supervised her care. Her belongings were routinely searched for blades. Clear orders were written regarding the level of nursing supervision required.If necessary, Rachel would receive one-to-one nursing from a 'special'. Contrary to the belief that individuals such as Rachel crave extra attention, the frequency of her presentations to hospital decreased and eventually stopped, although she continued with her outpatient treatment. (Hawton and van Heeringen 2000, p.544)

At the present time, there are two widely recognized classification systems for mental disorders, that is the DSM-IV-R (American Psychiatric Association 2000) and the ICD-10 (World Health Organisation 1992). These classification systems provide criteria for the identification of the different mental disorders, enabling diagnosis and treatment, identification and comparison of different groups of individuals. They are therefore important for clinical practice, research and statistical information. However, neither the DSM-IV-R nor the ICD-10 provides criteria for the diagnosis of deliberate self-harm.

As a result, a number of different terms have been put forward to describe suicidal behaviour, which has caused some confusion. For example, deliberate self-harm has been defined as 'causing deliberate hurt to your own body, most commonly by cutting, but also by burning, abusing drugs, alcohol or other substances' (Mental Health Foundation 2000). Another definition put forward by YoungMinds describes self-injury as 'a way of dealing with very difficult feelings that build up inside. People deal with these feelings in various ways. For example by cutting, burning or bruising themselves, taking an overdose of tablets, pulling hair or picking skin' (YoungMinds 2003, p.3).

The feeling of wanting to hurt myself would build up. I could put off doing it for a while but I couldn't last forever. (YoungMinds 2003, p.10)

Deliberate self-harm can also be referred to as self-injurious behaviour. Self-cutting or self-poisoning are more specific terms used to describe the behaviour. Self-cutting can often be used as a coping or self-management strategy. It can become habitual and is usually only visible when extreme. It is associated with depression, low self-esteem and sexual abuse. Usually people who self-harm in this way begin to do so at the age of 14 or 15 and may continue for a number of years. Self-poisoning is one of the most common reasons for admission into hospital in adolescents. In fact, research has found that the average annual death rate in the few years after discharge from hospital following an episode of self-poisoning was four times the national average annual death rate in adolescents of between 12 and 20 years of age (Goldacre and Hawton 1985; Hawton and Goldacre 1982).

The description and definition of another general term that is used, 'attempted suicide', has caused much debate. The unsatisfactory nature of the term has been criticized in that the majority of these patients are not in fact attempting suicide. As a result, the term 'parasuicide' has arisen, meaning an act that is like suicide, but is something other than suicide. Parasuicide was originally described by Kreitman (1977) and covers behaviours from 'suicidal gestures' or 'manipulative attempts' to more serious but unsuccessful attempts to kill oneself.

A definition of parasuicide was developed in order to include all forms of parasuicide for the World Health Organisation (WHO) European study on parasuicide. The definition states that parasuicide is 'an act with non-fatal outcome, in which an individual deliberately initiates a non-habitual behaviour that, without intervention from others, will cause self-harm, or deliberately ingests a substance in excess of the prescribed or generally recognised therapeutic dosage, and which is aimed at realising changes which the subject desired via the actual or expected physical consequences' (Hawton and van Heeringen 2000, p.51). However, the term 'parasuicide' has also been criticized for implying suicidal intention, when this may not in fact be present (Hawton and Catalan 1987).

Suicidal behaviour can also be conceptualized in terms of suicidal intent; whether the individual at the time of the episode of suicidal behaviour had a wish to die or whether the episode occurred without a wish to die in the secure belief that death would not occur as a result of their actions. Three categories therefore arise: individuals who want to die, individuals who do not want to die and those who are ambivalent as to whether they live or die (Hawton *et al.* 1982b). These groups can be conceptualized in diagrammatic form (see Figure 1.1).

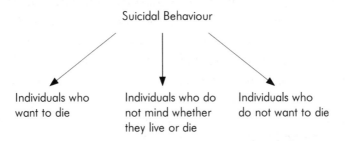

Figure 1.1 Different types of suicidal behaviour described in terms of motivation

Despite the confusion in terminology, deliberate self-harm is a widespread problem for clinical services. Until relatively recently, there was a lack of effective treatment interventions to reduce deliberate self-harm. There was no research to demonstrate an impact on repetition rates for a wide range of medical, social and psychological interventions (Hawton and Catalan 1987). However, within the last ten years a growing literature has emerged with respect to the empirical investigation of the psychological processes that underlie suicidal behaviour. This has been accompanied by the development of treatment interventions with the aim of reducing repetition rates in some high-risk groups.

Summary points

There are a number of myths that have arisen around the issue of deliberate self-harm; however, the reality portrays a very different picture. That is, people who engage in self-harming behaviour are not seeking attention, deliberate self-harm does hurt and the severity of the injury does not reflect the seriousness of the problem. The field of suicidal behaviour is also plagued with confusion with respect to the large number of different terms arising within the literature. For example, self-injurious behaviour, self-cutting, self-poisoning, attempted suicide, parasuicide. Neither DSM-IV-R nor ICD-10 provides diagnostic criteria for the identification of deliberate self-harm. In addition to the confusion in the terminology used to describe suicidal behaviour, suicidal behaviour can also be described in terms of suicidal intent, increasing the debate.

At the present time there is no consensus about the use of a common term and the confusion with terminology remains. For the purpose of this report a number of terms will be used consistently throughout. The term *suicidal behaviour* will encompass any form of intentional or deliberate self-injurious behaviour (suicide, attempted suicide, deliberate self-harm), although when referring to self-injurious behaviour that has a fatal outcome suicide will more often be used. *Deliberate self-harm* will refer to self-injurious behaviour with non-fatal outcome. Terms such as *deliberate self-cutting/injury* and *deliberate self-poisoning* will arise, depending on the method of deliberate self-harm used.

2 The Prevalence of Suicidal Behaviour in Adolescence

In order to investigate the question of how many people are affected by suicidal behaviour, prevalence figures need to be consulted. 'Prevalence' refers to the total number of cases of a disease or a disorder in a population at a specific point in time. It is only recently that epidemiological research has employed standardized procedures for the investigation of non-fatal suicidal behaviour. The lack of standardized procedures until recently has meant that there is a lack of exact figures on its prevalence.

In Europe, the USA and Australia a sharp increase was observed in the numbers of people treated because of self-injury or intentional overdose during the 1960s and 1970s (Hawton and Catalan 1987; Weissman 1974). The rates stabilized during the 1980s (Hawton and Fagg 1992; Platt *et al.* 1988), with a further increase in some catchment areas in the early 1990s (Hawton *et al.* 1997).

In England and Wales there are 142,000 admissions to accident and emergency departments each year (Hawton and Fagg 1992). However, this is a very small proportion of the total estimate of the number of people who engage in deliberate self-harm. In fact, it is estimated that one in 130 people, 446,000 or nearly half a million across the United Kingdom engage in deliberate self-harm each year (Mental Health Foundation website). It is estimated that approximately 25,000 adolescents present to general hospitals each year in England and Wales (Hawton *et al.* 2000). These figures arise because the episode of self-harm is not an attempt at fatal injury, but an attempt to inflict harm without the need for medical attention.

> Cutting was always a secret thing... You feel so ashamed, so bad about yourself. You feel no one will ever understand. (YoungMinds 2003, p.15)

Through recorded incidents of deliberate self-harm it is thought that women are three to four times more likely to exhibit self-harming behaviour than men and that it is also more commonly found in teenagers and young adults. Deliberate self-harm among children under the age of 12 is rare although it can occur. Four times as many girls than boys are thought to engage in deliberate self-harm. In hospital referred cases, the most common method of deliberate self-harm is self-poisoning, usually by an overdose of tablets. The other forms of self-harm such as cutting of wrists and arms are more often found in older adolescents and do not usually result in a serious threat to life. Between 40 and 100 times as many adolescents have engaged in deliberate self-harm compared to those who have actually ended their own lives.

Figures on deliberate self-harm have shown deviation in the numbers of adolescents engaging in self-harming behaviour since the 1960s. Deliberate self-harm (self-poisoning and self-injury) escalated in the late 1960s and early 1970s and was particularly common in adolescents (Hawton and Goldacre 1982). A decline in rates was observed in the late 1970s and early 1980s, especially in older teenage girls (Platt *et al.* 1988; Sellar, Hawton and Goldacre 1990). However, rates in older adolescent females were then noted to rise again in the late 1980s (Hawton and Fagg 1992). It appeared that between 1989 and 1992 the rates of deliberate self-harm in the United Kingdom were among the highest in Europe (Schmidtke *et al.* 1996).

Data relating to the prevalence of deliberate self-harm are available from different sources. Figures are usually taken from those who present for treatment at general hospitals, as described above. However, limitations of hospital bound studies mean that the number of people treated in general hospitals does not necessarily reflect the actual numbers of people who cause themselves harm. There are a number of reasons for this. Many acts of deliberate self-harm will not come to the attention of any medical professionals and in some countries episodes of deliberate self-harm are treated by a general practitioner and not by hospital staff. When patients do present to a hospital for treatment, there are no national registrations that reliably monitor trends in deliberate self-harmers. Other methodological limitations lie in the problematic definition of non-fatal suicidal behaviour, making it difficult to compare the results of epidemiological studies and the lack of comparison of the number of deliberate self-harmers with the catchment area of the particular hospital. That is to say, the number of people treated in a hospital for an episode of deliberate self-harm should be calculated against the size and characteristics of the population in the area that is served by the hospital.

Data are also available from community-based studies. There have been a large number of community-based studies concerning the prevalence of deliberate self-harm in adolescents in the general population, although the majority have been carried out in the USA or Europe (excluding the United Kingdom). Findings of the worldwide literature have been contradictory. There is also a lack of consistency within countries. For example, in the USA the lifetime prevalence of youth suicide has been reported to be between 3% (Lewis *et al*. 1988) and 30% (Dinges and Duong-Tran 1994). From community-based studies it is thought, however, that a median of 7 to 10% of adolescents attempt suicide (Safer 1997b).

Deliberate self-harm in adolescents: Oxford patient data

Hawton *et al*. (2000) used data collected by the Oxford Monitoring System for Attempted Suicide in order to look at teenage deliberate self-harm between 1985 and 1995. Data were collected on the basis of patients under 20 years of age presenting to the general hospital in Oxford with deliberate self-harm. The study highlighted an overall increase in the numbers of patients presenting with deliberate self-harm between 1985 and 1995 of 28.1% (27.7% in males and 28.3% in females). Repetition rates were also found to increase by 56.9% in males and 46.3% in females (49.4% overall).

During the study period (1985–1995), 1840 individuals under the age of 20 years presented to the general hospital in Oxford with deliberate self-harm. The numbers of individuals who presented with deliberate self-harm increased with age until the age of 18 where numbers levelled off, with a further increase at age 19. This could reflect the increased student population in the Oxford area however. There was a total of 1345 (73.1%) females and 495 (26.9%) males, showing a greater number of females engaging in deliberate self-harm (see Table 2.1 and Figure 2.1).

Table 2.1 Numbers of males and females by age at first presentation of deliberate self-harm in the Oxford region between 1985 and 1995

Age (years)	Males (n)	Females (n)	Total (n)
10	0	2	2
11	3	1	4
12	3	22	25
13	10	66	76
14	26	146	172
15	43	214	257
16	62	221	283
17	94	225	319
18	95	211	306
19	159	237	396
Total (n)	495	1345	1840

Repetition of deliberate self-harm was found to have increased between 1985 and 1995. The annual average episodes to person's ratio increased from 1:10 between 1985 and 1990 to 1:19 between 1991 and 1995. The increase in repetition was also reflected in the percentage of individuals repeating within a year of an episode. Between 1985 and 1989 the mean was 10.5% increasing to 14.0% between 1990 and 1994.

It was found that the most common method of deliberate self-harm was self-poisoning (88.7% overall). Seven and a half per cent were found to have presented with self-injury and 3.8% with both self-poisoning and self-injury. Self-injury was found to be more common in males than females (13.2% and 2.6% respectively). Conversely, females were more likely to have presented with self-poisoning than males (91.2% females, 82.5% males). For self-poisoning, an increase in the use of paracetamol was also noted.

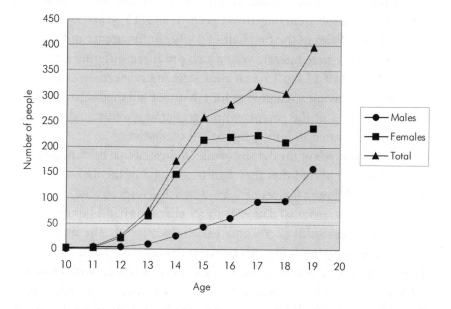

Figure 2.1 Numbers of males and females by age at first presentation of deliberate self-harm in the Oxford region between 1985 and 1995

Changes in the pattern of self-harm in Oxford have been shown to correlate highly with those in Edinburgh (Platt *et al.* 1988). Comparison of the recent trends observed in Oxford with those reported elsewhere indicates that they are representative of general trends of deliberate self-harm in the United Kingdom (Hawton and Goldacre 1982).

Deliberate self-harm in adolescents: national survey data
Meltzer *et al.* (2001)

A national survey of the mental health of children and adolescents in the United Kingdom (Meltzer *et al.* 2001) provided information on prevalence rates for a wide range of emotional, behavioural and hyperkinetic

disorders. Information was obtained for 10,438 (83%) children and adolescents aged between 5 and 15 years in the United Kingdom. Further
analysis of the data allows a more detailed look at children and adolescents who had ever attempted to harm, hurt or kill themselves. The data
presented below are taken from a report that came out of the original
survey that specifically focused on prevalence rates of self-harm among
children and adolescents aged between 5 and 15 years in England,
Scotland and Wales in the first half of 1999. Both parents and children
and adolescents were interviewed, which produced differing figures.

In total, 4249 11- to 15-year-olds were interviewed, of whom 248
reported ever having attempted to hurt, harm or kill themselves. In comparison, only 78 of the parents who were interviewed stated that their
child had attempted to hurt, harm or kill themselves.

Further analysis of the data by gender indicated that 6.5% of girls and
5.0% of boys reported that they had tried to harm themselves. Parents
reported much lower figures of 2.5% and 1.8% respectively.

According to parental data, 13- to 15-year-olds had $1\frac{1}{2}$ times the rate
of 11- to 12-year-olds (2.5% and 1.6% respectively). The highest rate
was reported by parents for girls between the ages of 13 and 15 at 3.1%.
These figures were also reflected in the children's reports with figures of
4.6% for 11- to 12-year-olds and 6.6% for 13- to 15-year-olds. Again,
the highest rates of self-harm were reported by girls between the ages of
13 and 15 years with a figure of 7.9%.

The prevalence of self-harm was higher among the children who had
a mental disorder compared to other 11- to 15-year-olds without a
mental illness. This was true for both reports given by parents (18.7% and
4.4% respectively) and the reports given by the children themselves
(10.1% and 1.2% respectively).

The prevalence of self-harm reported by parents was 18.8% for
children with depression, 12.6% for children with conduct disorder and
9.4% for children with an anxiety disorder. The prevalence of self-harm
was found to be higher when looking at the figures reported by the
children themselves: 37.4% for children with depression, 17.4% for
children with conduct disorder and 22% for children with an anxiety
disorder.

Other figures showed that self-harm was more prevalent where there were step children in the family compared to no step children. Prevalence rates of 3.7% and 1.9% respectively were obtained from parental report data and 8.4% and 5.5% respectively from child reports, indicating a similar pattern.

Self-harm was also found to be more prevalent where children came from lone parent families compared to two parent families. Rates of 3.1% of children from lone parent families and 1.8% of children from two parent families were reported to have engaged in self-harming behaviour according to parental reports and 6.7% and 5.5% respectively for child reports.

It was also found that the prevalence of self-harm was 6.2% from parental reports and 9.2% from children's reports for families where there were five or more children compared to 2.0% (parental reports) and 6.0% (children's reports) for families with two children. This indicates a higher prevalence of self-harm in families where there were five or more children compared to families where there were only one or two children.

The findings therefore suggest that the prevalence of self-harm is associated with gender, psychiatric profile and family characteristics.

Hawton et al. (2002)

Hawton *et al.* (2002) carried out a self-report survey in schools in England. This was a cross sectional survey using anonymous self-report questionnaires. Six thousand and twenty pupils aged 15 and 16 years from 41 schools in England took part.

Overall, 6.9% (398) of participants reported engaging in an act of self-harm (that met study criteria) in the previous year. Only 12.6% of episodes of self-harming behaviour had resulted in hospital presentation.

Deliberate self-harm was more common in females (11.2%) than in males (3.2%). The finding that deliberate self-harm is nearly four times as prevalent in females than males is similar to findings of hospital-based studies of this age group (Hawton *et al.* 2000).

Self-cutting (64.6%) and self-poisoning (30.7%) were the main methods used for deliberate self-harm. Of those adolescents who had self-poisoned, 22.9% had been referred to hospital, compared to 6.3% for self-cutting.

Factors associated with self-harming behaviour in females were suicidal behaviour by friends or family members, drug misuse, anxiety, depression, impulsivity and low self-esteem. In males factors included self-harm by friends or family, drug use and low self-esteem.

Multiple acts of deliberate self-harm were reported by 54% of participants who had engaged in self-harming behaviour (218 of 398).

Higher rates of deliberate self-harm were found in females living with one parent whether or not a step parent and deliberate self-harm was found to be less common in Asian than white females.

Deliberate self-harm is a common reason for which adolescents present to hospital. Community studies conducted outside the United Kingdom have shown that there is a much greater prevalence of self-harming behaviour in adolescents than the findings of hospital studies have shown (Choquet and Ledoux 1994; Kann *et al.* 2000). This study supports this notion, in particular for adolescent females. The study suggests that awareness of recent self-harming behaviour in peers and family members, drug misuse, impulsivity, anxiety, depression and low self-esteem are important associated factors.

Summary points

Figures describing rates of suicidal behaviour for Europe, the USA and Australia portray a sharp increase in the numbers of people treated for self-injury in the 1960s and 1970s, which stabilized during the 1980s. A further increase was subsequently observed in some catchment areas in the early 1990s. Figures show that women are three to four times more likely than men to engage in self-harming behaviour, it is most commonly found in teenagers and young adults, it is rare in children under the age of 12 and the most common method in hospital referred cases is self-poisoning. However, data relating to the prevalence of deliberate self-harm are thought to underestimate the size of the problem. This is owing to inconsistencies in the way terms are defined and data are collected and coded and the fact that not all cases of suicidal behaviour will require hospital care. The identification of a death as suicide is also subjective in nature. As a result, care needs to be taken in the interpretation of figures on the prevalence of suicidal behaviour.

3 Risk Factors for Adolescent Suicidal Behaviour

> I think control's a big thing. You can't control what's happening around you, but you can control what you do to yourself.
>
> (Spandler 1996, p.34)

People usually self-harm at times of extreme anger, distress and low self-esteem. Deliberate self-harm can be a form of punishment, serve to create a physical manifestation of the negative feelings that the person has, which can then be dealt with or even result from a sense of hopelessness that the person may have.

One of the most challenging and troublesome areas for research into suicidal behaviour is to find out why it occurs. This is particularly true in the case of research that is strongly evidenced-based because scientific study will only identify factors that contribute to suicidal behaviour from which reasons can be inferred.

Many risk factors have been identified and discussed in the literature that relate to suicidal behaviour. Causality however, has been based on the assumption that risk factors are associated with each other, with no one causal factor having been identified. Beautrais (1998) discusses methodological problems with research into the causal factors of suicidal behaviour, and concludes that the research area is so problematic that it is possible to examine research into almost any area of adolescent suicide and argue that no clear conclusions can be drawn owing to problematic design. However, what empirical work has shown is that some of these risk factors appear to play very important roles.

Although evidence needs to be strengthened in order to gain a better understanding of the complexity of the interaction between risk factors, there is consistency in many studies, providing a basis for informed judgements about suicide risk (Beautrais 1998). Evidence suggests that suicidal behaviour is related to complex and confounding vulnerabilities and is not just a response to a single stressor. No one risk factor is the cause therefore, but it is the outcome of a build-up of stressors in a person with few protective factors and whose resilience is poor.

In fact, people can become stressed for a number of reasons, for example, bullying, bereavement, housing problems, abuse, problems to do with race, culture or religion, growing up, money, pressure to fit in, sexual feelings, problems with friends or pressures at school or at work. If a number of these problems occur at the same time then things can become too much and if the person already feels vulnerable then they will find it hard to cope.

Causes and correlates of suicidal behaviour that have been put forward include: illness (mental or physical illness, including drug or alcohol abuse), personal factors (social support and attitudes towards suicide), stressful life events (loss of job, bereavement), the wider cultural environment (changes in economic climate, cultural attitudes) and access to methods (easy access to lethal means) (Charlton, Kelly and Dunnell 1993).

Factors that have more specifically been linked to non-fatal suicidal behaviour (deliberate self-harm/injury) include:

- parental problems (criminality, reliance on welfare benefits)
- a disrupted upbringing (periods of local authority care, parental marital problems such as separation or divorce)
- ongoing family relationship problems
- mental health problems of the child (hopelessness and depression).

The psychological autopsy has been an accepted method used in the investigation of mental and psychosocial characteristics of suicide victims for 30 years. This was initially used with adult populations, but has subsequently been found to be of use in studies specifically focusing on adolescents (Brent *et al.* 1988b; Marttunen *et al.* 1991; Shafii *et al.* 1985; Shafii *et al.* 1988). The majority of the research utilizing this approach has been carried out in the USA. Results have indicated that risk factors for suicide in children and adolescents include having a psychiatric disorder, in particular an affective or mood disorder, previous attempts and substance and/or alcohol abuse (Shaffer *et al.* 1996; Shafii *et al.* 1988). Little research has used the psychological autopsy in studying adolescents in the United Kingdom, however (for example, Houston, Hawton and Shepperd 2001; Shaffer 1974).

Models of suicidal behaviour

The psychodynamic approach

Research has highlighted a number of psychological mechanisms that contribute to the triggering of suicidal crises. Psychodynamic models have been put forward and various personality variables and cognitive factors discussed. Although Freud never wrote a paper that specifically addressed the issue of suicide, his paper *Mourning and Melancholia* (1917) has been influential. The paper compared severe depression with the normal experience of mourning following the loss of a loved one. Freud believed that the majority of individuals would be able to cope, but that other vulnerable individuals would find the loss experience unbearable, which would cause the generation of a lot of anger.

This causes ambivalence, but the person preserves the mental image of the loved one by internalizing it so that it becomes part of the ego. The inability to express the feelings of anger towards the loved one causes the feelings to be transformed into feelings of self-blame and wanting to harm oneself. Stillion and McDowell (1996) highlight other relevant issues in Freud's later writings. Freud proposed the existence of two energy forces – Eros and Thanatos – which are in constant dynamic balance. Eros was seen as the life force, driving towards survival, while Thanatos was seen as the death instinct. There was a constant interplay between these two forces throughout an individual's life. Threatening thoughts or experiences are repressed in the unconscious, leaving less energy available for growth and development. This risks the life force, Eros, being overwhelmed by the death force, Thanatos. Suicide is therefore conceptualized by Freud as the result of an intra-psychic struggle. Other researchers have developed Freud's ideas, for example Zilboorg (1937) who included revenge, fear, spite and fantasies of escape as triggers for suicide, and suggested that most suicides are impulsive acts. In fact, many of the early themes put forward by psychodynamic theory can be found in much later empirical work.

'Cry of pain' model of suicidal behaviour

Williams (1997) put forward a model that postulates that suicidal behaviour should be conceptualized as a 'cry of pain'. The individual is trying to escape from a situation within which they feel they have been 'defeated'. These feelings of defeat may result from external influences such as unemployment, job stress or poor relationships or inner turmoil. The individual feels that they are trapped in a situation where there is nothing that they can do to escape and no one can help them. The 'cry of pain' model therefore describes a combination of circumstances where the person perceives themselves to have been defeated, with no way of escape or rescue and where the means by which they may harm themselves is available.

This model accounts for both non-lethal self-harm, more lethal suicidal behaviour and suicide. It states that a person is sensitive to the degree to which there is 'escape potential' from a stressful situation. Less serious self-harming behaviour therefore represents an attempt to re-establish escape routes. More lethal suicidal behaviour and completed suicide are seen as a 'cry of pain' where the person perceives there to be no escape routes and no possibility of rescue. In this case the person feels completely 'defeated'. This model emphasizes that suicidal behaviour is 'reactive', elicited by a combination of circumstances, rather than 'communicative', seen as a cry for help.

Personal characteristics as risk factors

Problem-solving

Deficits in problem-solving are a psychological characteristic that has been observed in adult suicide attempters (McCleavy *et al.* 1987; Schotte and Clum 1987). If suicidal behaviour is seen to be associated with feeling that there is no escape from their present circumstances, then impairment in the ability to solve problems will play an important role. In fact, several studies have found important differences in the problem-solving of suicidal individuals when compared to controls. For example, deficient problem-solving skills of adolescents following an overdose such as poor problem orientation and maladaptive affect in response to problems (Sadowski and Kelly 1993) have been demonstrated. The generation of fewer alternatives for solving problems, greater focus on the problem rather than a potential solution and more wishful thinking have also been found in adolescents following an episode of self-poisoning (Rotheram-Borus and Trautman 1990). Similarly, Orbach, Bar-Joseph and Dror (1990) found that adolescents who had harmed themselves tended to depend more on others, were less versatile and less relevant in their problem-solving. Solutions of those who had harmed themselves also made less reference to the future than solutions of non-suicidal patients. Young people between the ages of 13 and 18 years who have a history of a previous overdose and/or who repeated self-harm during the following year have been shown to have lower scores for self-rated problem-solving and effectiveness of problem-solving than non-repeaters (Hawton *et al.* 1999).

Impulsivity

Another characteristic that has been investigated is that of impulsivity. Much of the research on impulsivity has in fact been in adolescents. It appears to be a common feature within this population and has been found to characterize self-poisoners independently of depression (Kingsbury *et al.* 1999). For example, a study carried out by Hawton *et al.* (1982b) found that self-poisoning in a sample of adolescents who presented to a general hospital described it as an impulsive act. Half of the 50 adolescent self-poisoners who were interviewed stated that they had only seriously thought about the act for less than 15 minutes beforehand.

Eight stated that they had thought about it for between 15 minutes and one hour, with only four contemplating taking an overdose for more than 24 hours. In another study, Kerfoot *et al.* (1996) found that in most cases the overdoses were unplanned with only 20% showing evidence of planning for more than three hours before. Similarly, Pfeffer *et al.* (1988) found that adolescents with a tendency towards explosive and aggressive behaviour were at greater risk for repetition of suicidal behaviour. An increased risk of suicidal behaviour has also been noted in children and adolescents where there is impulsivity or a lack of concern for danger found in their histories (Shafii and Shafii 1982).

In another study investigating adolescent suicide, Hawton *et al.* (1982a) found that most adolescent suicides are unplanned and other studies have found that only 25% of completed suicides by adolescents show some evidence of planning. Most adolescent suicides are impulsive acts (Hoberman and Garfinkel 1988; Shaffer *et al.* 1988). In a study of adolescent suicides, Shaffer (1974) found that impulsivity, perfectionism, tendency to withdraw and aloofness were associated personality features.

Hopelessness

Suicidal behaviours in children and adolescents have been consistently associated with depressive symptoms and disorders (Kovacs, Goldston and Gatsonis 1993). For example, Brent *et al.* (1993b) found that where inpatient adolescents received a diagnosis of depression at admission and six-month follow-up, this was a strong predictor of suicidal behaviour. In fact, depression has been found to be one of the best predictors for adolescent suicidal behaviour (Garrison *et al.* 1991). However, other variables are likely to mediate the relationship between depression and suicidal behaviour. Hopelessness has also been found to be associated with suicidal ideation and suicidal behaviour in some adolescent patient samples (Kazdin *et al.* 1983). Suicidal children have been found to be more hopeless than non-suicidal children (Pfeffer *et al.* 1979), a finding supported by Marciano and Kazdin (1994) who found greater depression, hopelessness and lower self-esteem in suicidal children compared to non-suicidal children. Kashani *et al.* (1991) also found that more hopeless children were more suicidal. Kerfoot *et al.* (1996) looked at the correlates of self-poisoning in adolescents and found that suicidal ideation and hopelessness were significantly higher in the overdose cases than in the controls.

Anger and hostility

Some studies have investigated anger and hostility. Research has found that young suicide attempters are more hostile than community controls (Simonds, McMahon and Armstrong 1991). Apter *et al.* (1988) investigated adolescent psychiatric inpatients and found that those with conduct disorder had more suicidal feelings than those diagnosed with major depression. Similarly, Hawton *et al.* (1982c) found a much higher repetition rate in adolescent self-poisoners with antisocial behaviour than adolescent self-poisoners without a history of antisocial behaviour. Fifty per cent of adolescents who had a history of antisocial behaviour and who took an overdose repeated within a year.

Psychiatric disorders as risk factors

Mental health problems carry an increased risk of both fatal and non-fatal suicidal behaviour. Beautrais, Joyce and Mulder (1998) carried out a case-control study of 129 suicide attempters and 153 controls aged between 13 and 25 years. The study investigated psychiatric illness in young people making serious suicide attempts in New Zealand. They found that 89.5% of patients exhibiting suicidal behaviour had a current mental disorder. Comorbidity of disorders was found in 54.3% of patients, with 90.7% having a lifetime history of psychiatric disorder. There were a number of methodological problems with this study, however. First, cases were significantly younger than the controls and no matching techniques were used to control for other differences such as socio-economic status, background, race/ethnicity, method of attempt etc., which may have had an effect on the outcome. Second, cases presented to an emergency department and needed to be admitted for a 24-hour period, limiting the generalizability of the results to only the more serious cases of adolescent suicide. Third, it is also important to keep in mind the method of data collection; information was obtained through interviewing patients themselves and a significant other. Human recall can have limitations and may be biased, leading to over/underestimation of events. There was some recognition of this, however, through questioning a significant other, in order to confirm information obtained. The reliability of the psychiatric morbidity was also checked through test-retest methods and controls were selected from electoral roles for the area in which the hospital was located. In addition, the results of this study are in line with other research (for example, Brent *et al.* 1988a, 1993b; Marttunen *et al.* 1991; Shaffer *et al.* 1988; Shafii *et al.* 1988).

Similarly, Garnefski and Diekstra (1995) carried out a case-control study of 477 patients with a history of suicidal behaviour and 477 controls, aged between 12 and 19 years. The study investigated suicidal behaviour and the co-occurrence of behavioural, emotional and cognitive problems among adolescents. The study found that non-attempters were more likely to have a problem in a 'single' psychiatric category, whereas suicide attempters were found to have more problems in 'multiple' psychiatric categories. They also noted that the number of cognitive, emotional and behavioural problems seemed to be of more importance in relation to a history of suicidal behaviour than the specific problem type. There are a number of methodological issues with this study. First, information was obtained through a self-report questionnaire with no well-documented medical records to back up the data. Human recall can be limited and with no information used as confirmation it seems likely that recall bias is operating here. Second, patients represented white secondary school students limiting generalizability of the results of the study to other populations. Despite these limitations, however, the control group came from the same population as the cases and seem to only have differed in not having made a suicide attempt. Participants were also matched on age, school, type of education and gender. The sample size used within this study was good and the authors do acknowledge the limitations of using a self-report questionnaire. The finding that co-morbidity of disorders is found in adolescents who engage in suicidal behaviour is also supported by more recent work (Houston *et al.* 2001; Kerfoot *et al.* 1996).

An increasing body of evidence is emerging that supports links between suicidal behaviour and depression, antisocial behaviour and substance abuse (Kerfoot 1996). Gould *et al.* (1998) found that mood, anxiety and substance abuse/dependence disorders independently increased the risk of suicide attempts. In addition, associations between suicidal behaviour and cognitive and/or emotional problems such as low self-esteem and depressed mood have been established within secondary school populations (Clark 1993; Garrison 1989; Kienhorst *et al.* 1990a; Lewinsohn, Rohde and Seeley 1993; Pronovost, Cote and Ross 1990; Rubenstein *et al.* 1989; Smith 1990; Smith and Crawford 1986; Spirito *et al.* 1989). Others have found an association with behavioural problems such as substance abuse and aggressive or criminal behaviour (Andrews and Lewinsohn 1992; Dubow *et al.* 1989; Garnefski, Diekstra and de Heus 1992; Kienhorst *et al.* 1990b; Lewinsohn *et al.* 1993; Smith 1990; Spirito *et al.* 1989).

Psychological autopsy studies have reported figures of psychiatric disorder in adolescents who commit suicide of about 90% (Brent *et al.* 1988a, 1993b; Marttunen *et al.* 1991; Shaffer *et al.* 1988; Shafii *et al.* 1988). Diagnoses have included affective disorders, substance misuse and personality disorders (Marttunen *et al.* 1991). Brent *et al.* (1993c) found that prominent psychiatric diagnoses were major depression (43%), conduct disorder (28%) and substance abuse (27%). Similarly, Shaffer *et al.* (1996) found that frequent psychiatric diagnostic groups were mood disorders, disruptive disorders such as conduct disorder and substance and alcohol abuse. There has been less consensus as to the type of psychiatric disorder most closely associated with adolescent suicide, however. Some find substance abuse and antisocial disorder to be the most common psychiatric diagnoses (Rich, Sherman and Fowler 1990; Rich, Young and Fowler 1986), while others report affective illness to be the most frequent (Brent *et al.* 1988a; Shafii *et al.* 1988). Brent *et al.* (1993b) reported that the biggest diagnostic risk factor was major depression. They also found elevated levels of substance abuse and conduct disorder, however. Houston *et al.* (2001) investigated the risk of suicidal behaviour posed by mental health problems through the use of the psychological autopsy method. They investigated the suicides of 27 young people aged between 15 and 24. Psychiatric illness was present in

70.4% of subjects. Affective disorders were found to be the predominant psychiatric diagnosis. Personality disorders were present in more than a quarter of subjects. However, substance abuse was relatively uncommon, although often reported as common in other studies. Nearly all of the subjects were also experiencing multiple problems at the time of death, with mental health problems most frequently judged to have contributed to the suicide (59.3%).

Comorbidity of psychiatric disorders also seems to be common in adolescents who commit suicide or who exhibit suicidal behaviour (Houston *et al.* 2001; Kerfoot *et al.* 1996).

Depression

Depression has been found to be one of the most common psychiatric diagnoses in adolescents who deliberately self-harm. Research suggests that children who have harmed themselves have many features in common with depressed children (de Wilde *et al.* 1993; Pfeffer 1992). Some researchers have found that the outcome of deliberate self-harm is similar to that of childhood depression (Lewinsohn, Rohde and Seeley 1994) and that repetition of deliberate self-harm is often linked to episodes of depression (Pfeffer *et al.* 1993). It may be easy to conceptualize deliberate self-harm in the context of these findings as a symptom of major depressive disorder. However, Kerfoot *et al.* (1996) argue against this stating that depression has a different significance when it occurs in the context of deliberate self-harm. Their research suggests that major depressive disorder often remits following deliberate self-harm.

Kerfoot *et al.* (1996) found that 67% of adolescents who had self-poisoned had a diagnosis of major depressive disorder. In addition, Burgess *et al.* (1998) followed up adolescent self-poisoners and found high levels of psychopathology; 72% of the adolescents had a diagnosable psychiatric disorder, 48% with major depression. Furthermore, Hawton *et al.* (1999) have shown that young people between the ages of 13 and 18 years who have a history of a previous overdose and/or who repeated self-harm during the following year have higher scores on standardized measures for depression and hopelessness, and lower scores for self-esteem, than non-repeaters. Risk factors identified for non-fatal repetition include male gender, a history of previous attempts, depressive symptomatology, poor communication and hopelessness (Choquet and Menke 1990; Pfeffer *et al.* 1991; Sellar *et al.* 1990).

Shaffer *et al.* (1996) investigated psychiatric diagnosis in adolescents who had committed suicide and found a diagnosis of major depressive disorder in 52%. Retrospective examination of information about individuals who have killed themselves has led to estimates of up to 70% of people who suffer from depression thought to have committed suicide. Another study carried out by Brent *et al.* (1993b) found that 31% of adolescent suicide victims had an onset of major depressive disorder only three months previous to death, with 41.4% having onset six months previous and 48.3% 12 months previous to death. In fact, depression has been termed the 'final common pathway' to suicide (Williams and Pollock 1993).

In support of these findings, Myers *et al.* (1991) found that depressive thinking was one of the most powerful predictors of suicide. They carried out a study of 100 patients with major depressive disorder and 38 psychiatric controls aged between 7 and 17 years. This study had a fairly robust methodology. Information was obtained through interviewing subjects using the KIDDIE-SADS. Inter-rater reliability was checked and interviewers were blind to the children's diagnoses. The control group consisted of patients from the same population, that is, psychiatric patients who did not have depressive symptoms. No significant differences were found for age, sex, race/ethnicity or socio-economic status between cases and controls. The authors investigated a large number of variables including, diagnosis, severity of depression, suicidality status, comorbidity, life-stress, youth self-perception, and parental factors such as diagnosis, suicidality status and generalized psychopathology. Cases and controls were recruited from inpatient and outpatient services at a teaching hospital, increasing the generalizability of results and the study had a large sample size. It is important to note, however, that subjects were from middle- and upper-class backgrounds and were predominantly of white ethnic origin, meaning that it is not possible to generalize results beyond these populations.

Substance abuse

Alcohol and drug use is common in people who have attempted suicide. Alcohol is often used immediately before or during a suicide attempt, increasing the likelihood of death. Alcohol use at the time of the act has been found to be common in both males and females (Kerfoot 1988).

A history of substance abuse is also found in adolescent suicide. Following attempted suicide, substance abuse is a key risk factor for subsequent suicide. Alcohol and drugs are particularly implicated in suicides among young men where impulsiveness is a factor in the decision to act. One study found that 16.7% of adolescent suicides had an onset of substance abuse within the 12 months before death, with a mean onset of 35.6 months before death (Brent *et al.* 1993b).

A similar finding was presented by Jones (1997). In this study suicidal adolescents reported more drug and alcohol use than a control group. The study suffered a number of methodological limitations, however. It had a small sample size; only 15 suicide attempters and 15 non-suicide attempters aged between 12 and 17 years took part, limiting the power of the results. Adolescents were interviewed in order to ascertain suicidal intent, lethality, psychiatric symptomatology and family psychiatric history. This information was not backed up by well-documented medical records however, and as a result there may have been an under-representation of substance abuse, for example the amount and frequency. It is difficult to know whether recall bias was operating, although given the method of data collection it may have been in this case. Cases presented to the psychiatric emergency clinic and controls were recruited from a paediatric emergency clinic at the same hospital for minor illnesses. Cases and controls were matched on age and gender. All participants were of African American origin and were from an urban, low socio-economic status background, limiting the generalizability of the results.

In another study, Cavaiola and Lavender (1999) investigated suicidal behaviour in chemically dependent adolescents. Their study had a larger sample size, a total of 150 participants: 50 suicide attempters who were chemically dependent, 50 non-suicide attempters who were chemically dependent and 50 non-suicidal non-chemically dependent high school controls. They found that a suicidal group of adolescents were more psychologically distressed than non-suicidal, chemically dependent and non-suicidal non-chemically dependent adolescents. Significant differences were also found between the suicidal and non-suicidal chemically dependent groups in terms of somatization, depression, anxiety and phobic anxiety. There are a number of methodological issues to keep in mind in the interpretation of these results. First, information was obtained from interviews with subjects and their families. It is therefore important to keep in mind the limitations of human recall, which could have led to under reporting during interviews. Recall bias may also cause a particular problem given the emotional aspect of suicidal behaviour for the patient and their family. Other variables might have had an effect on the outcome, including: gender, race/ethnicity, socio-economic status. Little discussion of the characteristics of each of the groups was given, however, so it is difficult to tell whether these variables had been taken into account. Cases were chemically dependent adolescents taken from a specialized treatment programme, therefore limiting the generalizability of results to other populations. Nevertheless, two control groups were used in this study, one of which was taken from the same population at the treatment centre but who were not suicidal and the other from schools in the local community area.

Conduct disorder

Certain groups show a considerably higher risk of deliberate self-harm than the general population. For example, one third of people supervised by the West Yorkshire Probation Service were found to have a history of deliberate self-harm (Wessely *et al.* 1996). Aggressive behaviour and stressful experiences in boys and delinquent behaviour in girls have also been found to be good predictors of suicidal behaviour (Achenbach *et al.* 1995). Young people between the ages of 13 and 18 years with a history of a previous overdose and/or who repeated self-harm during the following year, have been found to exhibit higher scores on standardized measures for trait anger (Hawton *et al.* 1999) and antisocial and behavioural problems have been found to be present (Kerfoot 1988).

Renaud *et al.* (1999) investigated suicide in adolescents with disruptive disorders. They looked at demographic characteristics, details of the suicide, disruptive disorder details, comorbid psychiatric disorders, past suicidal behaviour and ideation, life events, family history of psychiatric disorder. The study found that adolescents with disruptive disorders are at risk of suicide when comorbid substance abuse and a past history of suicide are present. However, the study had a relatively small sample size: 59 suicide completers (mean age 17.4 years) and 18 community controls (mean age 17.1 years). It is unclear how cases were identified and from where. Information was obtained through interviewing, so recall bias may be operating and information recalled may be limited. The authors did use multiple informants in order to try and obtain some sort of consensus on information obtained, however. The control group consisted of individuals with disruptive disorder who had not committed suicide from the community and were of a similar age, race, gender, socio-economic status and county of residence, limiting bias. A number of other variables were investigated, including: demographic characteristics, characteristics of the suicide, characteristics of the disruptive disorders, psychiatric disorders, past suicidal behaviour, firearms, life events and family history of psychiatric disorder. It is unclear as to what kind of population the cases represent as little detail is given about how subjects were recruited and where from. This proves problematic in the generalizability of results. Nevertheless, results are in line with other research.

For example, Feldman and Wilson (1997) also highlighted a link between conduct disorder and suicidal behaviour. They found that a suicidal group of adolescents with a conduct disorder diagnosis scored lower on the Epigenetic Assessment Rating System (EARS) (Wilson, Passik and Kuras 1989) than non-psychiatric patients. They scored lower on dimensions measuring affect tolerance, affect expression and use of an object. The EARS and the Children's Depression Inventory (CDI) (Kovacs 1982; Kovacs and Beck 1977) each identified a different subset of suicidal adolescents. That is, although depression was found in fewer than half the suicidal adolescents, there were a substantial number of suicidal, but not depressed adolescents with conduct disorder. It is important for clinicians not to rely on the assumed link between suicide and depression therefore. They also noted that lower EARS scores lead to a greater reactivity to separation experiences on the Separation Anxiety Test (SAT) (Hansburg 1980a, 1980b). Participants were recruited from a large municipal hospital. However, the use of community controls eliminated factors specific to the hospital that might affect the results. Information on suicidal behaviour was taken from emergency room notes and treatment team notes, so that information was not based on human recall. Controls were recruited from non-psychiatric community groups living nearby. Subjects were matched by age, sex, race and socio-economic status. No significant differences were found between the groups on any of these variables. Other variables that may have had an effect on the results include: repetition of suicidal behaviour (previous episodes), the method of suicide and other psychiatric variables such as number of inpatient stays, length of stay, history of diagnoses etc., none of which were investigated. The study involved an urban minority population, which limits the generalizability of results to other populations.

Psychological autopsy research has investigated the life history of subjects, which has often suggested long-standing difficulties. For example, one study found that nearly half of subjects had exhibited emotional and/or behavioural problems during childhood or adolescence, with nearly half having been in trouble with the police. Another study found that 11.1% of adolescent suicide victims had an onset of conduct disorder within 12 months before death, with a mean onset of 45.9 months before death (Brent *et al.* 1993b).

Family risk factors

A number of family risk factors for suicidal behaviour have been identified. Over half of children under the age of 16 who present with deliberate self-harm live with only one parent due to separation or divorce, and 40% will have spent some time in local authority care. Disturbed family relationships are also common, especially among girls and for older teenagers. Hollis (1996) found that depressive syndrome, family discord, disturbed mother-child relationship and a lack of warmth in the family were each independently associated with suicidal behaviour. Adolescent self-poisoners have been found to present with more interpersonal problems such as poor peer relationships than community controls. They are also more likely to come from dysfunctional families that are often on benefits (Kerfoot *et al.* 1996).

Psychological autopsy research investigating adolescent suicide has highlighted a number of family risk factors. One study found that approximately a quarter of subjects had experienced family instability or poverty, although the majority did not come from broken homes. In addition, a quarter had been exposed to suicidal behaviour by a family member, and half came from families with a history of psychiatric disorder. Disruption in the relationship with a partner was also found to be an important contributing factor (44.4%) (Houston *et al.* 2001). Brent *et al.* (1993c) looked at the relationship between family history of mental disorder and mental illness in suicide victims. They demonstrated a relationship between diagnosis in the suicide victim and the family members. The mental illness diagnosis of each subject was associated with an increased risk of a diagnosis of the same disorder in first-degree relatives (siblings, mothers and fathers). This was true for suicidal victims diagnosed with bipolar spectrum disorder, conduct disorder and substance abuse. In particular, the family history of suicide victims diagnosed with substance abuse showed an increase in rates of affective disorder, major depression and substance abuse.

It appears that the interaction of the personal characteristics of the individual and their environment plays a key role in the development of suicidal behaviour, with the exposure to environmental stressors, the perceived meaning of the stressors and the behavioural reaction of the person to the stressors all forming an important part in this interaction.

The media

Research has found that suicidal behaviour can be learnt through imitation. This is especially true for children, adolescents and young adults (Diekstra 1974; Kreitman, Smith and Tan 1970; Platt 1993; Schmidtke 1988, 1996; Schmidtke and Schaller 1998; Steede and Range 1989; Velting and Gould 1997). The mass media has been hypothesized to provide a mode of transmission of models for imitation. Research has looked at different methods of presentation such as print media (literature and press), music, broadcasting, television, film, theatre and electronic media such as the Internet. For example, one book, *Final Exit* (Humphry 2002) recommended asphyxiation as a method for committing suicide. Stack (1999) found that in the year that the book was published suicide by asphyxiation increased in New York City by 313% and in 27.3% of the cases a copy of the book was found to be present at the scene (Marzuk *et al.* 1993, 1994; Stack 1999). Similarly, a study carried out by Phillips (1974) found that the more publicity that a suicide case was given, the more suicides there were in the period following the publication. Other studies have found similar trends (Hassan 1995; Hills 1995; Sonneck, Etzersdorfer and Nagel-Kuess 1994), although some research has provided contradictory findings questioning the 'copycat effect' (Jonas 1992; Kessler *et al.* 1988; Wasserman 1993).

Research that has focused on media portrayal of suicidal behaviour and the effect that it has on young people has provided substantial evidence that reporting of suicidal behaviour in newspapers can be a contributory factor to suicidal behaviours in young people (Hawton and Williams 2001; Pirkis and Blood 2001; Schmidtke and Schaller 2000). Martin (1996) investigated the influence that the portrayal of suicide on television had on a sample of 14-year-old students taken from the general population. Those students who claimed that they had been exposed to suicide shown on television more than twice were found to differ from their age peers without such exposure. They took more risks, were more prone to substance abuse, had higher depression scores, knew more 'real-life suicides' and were more likely to have a history of deliberate self-harm. This study has been criticized, however, for not making clear whether the suicides were real or fictional. The relationship between reports of exposure to suicidal behaviour on television and deliberate self-harm was also found to no longer reach statistical significance when knowledge of someone who had committed suicide was controlled for.

Another study supporting the 'copycat effect' was carried out by Ostroff *et al.* (1985). They reported an increase in attempted suicide following the showing of a television film that depicted the suicide of a young couple and the effect that it had on their parents.

Similarly, Wilson and Hunter (1983) reported an increase in the occurrence of suicide in the USA following the broadcast of a television series entitled *Death of a Student.* Schmidtke and Hafner (1988) also investigated the imitation effect following the broadcasting of the same television series. They used a 'natural single-case-experiment' replication design. The series comprised of six episodes and was shown in German in 1981. At the start of each episode, the lethal outcome of a railway suicide by a 19-year-old male was shown, and the beginning of the suicidal act was shown in episodes two to six. The series was then shown again on television in 1982. They found that there was an increase in railway suicides. This was particularly true in the case of young men. An increase of 86% in suicides of young males was observed during the 70 days after the first broadcasting of the series (figures were compared to the means for the previous year). Elevated numbers of suicides were also noted for a period of 16 weeks for 15- to 19-year-old males and ten weeks for 20- to 24-year-old males. The effect on suicides was less marked following the broadcasting of the series for a second time, although increases in the numbers of railway suicides by young men corresponded to viewing figures for the first and second showings of the series.

Two reviews of the world literature on suicide and media influence have found compelling evidence of an association between presentations of suicide and attempted suicide in newspapers, on television and in books and subsequent suicidal behaviour in young people (Hawton and Williams 2001; Pirkis and Blood 2001). It was also demonstrated that this effect was more likely where the portrayal was dramatic, methods were specified, where it involved celebrities and where it was repeated.

Summary points

Investigation into the risk factors for suicidal behaviour proves both challenging and troublesome. In fact, many factors have been identified that are thought to increase the risk of suicidal behaviour. It is assumed that causality lies with an association between risk factors. Risk factors that have been put forward include: deficits in problem-solving, impulsivity, feelings of hopelessness, anger and hostility, having a psychiatric disorder, family characteristics such as lone parent families and disturbed family relationships and the media.

Research has found links between suicidal behaviour and depression, substance abuse and conduct disorder; however, empirical work tends to suffer from small sample sizes, a lack of generalizability of results and limitations owing to methods of data collection. Future research will need to assume a more robust methodology in order to make any firm conclusions about links between suicidal behaviour and depression, substance abuse and conduct disorder in the adolescent population.

There is substantial evidence that reporting of suicidal behaviour in newspapers can be a contributory factor to suicidal behaviours in young people. The media should make the association between mental health problems and suicidal behaviour clear and any reports should be accompanied by information on how to access sources of help.

Although research has been consistent in the results obtained, much of the research is problematic, leaving an area requiring further investigation.

4 Identifying At-Risk Adolescents

Attention to the identification of young people who have engaged in suicidal behaviour or who are at risk of engaging in suicidal behaviour has increased over the last few years. This is in part owing to the increase in awareness of suicidal behaviour as a problem, but also to suicide being the third leading cause of death among young people. One of the best predictors of adolescent suicide is a previous suicide attempt (Leon *et al.* 1990; Shafii *et al.* 1985). Other risk factors must not be neglected however. This is because only between 10 and 40% of adolescents who commit suicide have made a previous attempt (Brent *et al.* 1988a; Marttunen, Aro and Lonnqvist 1993). When assessing for the risk of suicide it is important to look at intent, lethality, precipitants and motivation. The assessment of intent includes self-report measures and notation of the circumstances of the act. It is often the case however that an attempted suicide is a highly impulsive act. Suicidal behaviour is often linked to a clear precipitant, for example an event or circumstance, which has caused a crisis for the individual. This could have occurred suddenly or have been building up over a long period of time. The identification of at-risk adolescents may prove particularly difficult. Adolescents have been found to provide discrepant information and are reluctant to give personal information to an adult, who is seen as an authority figure (Brent *et al.* 1988a; Velting, Rathus and Asnis 1998).

According to Shaffer *et al.* (1988), initiatives for the prevention of suicidal behaviour in schools that focus on screening for vulnerable populations would be more profitable compared to peer group 'buddying' schemes, or peer surveillance. Others believe that screening procedures to detect adolescents who are at risk for suicidal behaviour should focus more on multiple patterns of emotional, behavioural and cognitive problems than to single problems (Garnefski and Diekstra 1995).

Screening instruments for the identification of at-risk individuals

From 1994, a series of workshops was organized in the USA, sponsored by the National Institute of Mental Health with various other organizations. The workshops focused on problems of the classification of suicidal behaviour, the need for consensus in the assessment of suicidality and knowledge regarding the utility of measures of suicidality. As a result of these workshops, a review of the instruments used to assess suicidal behaviours and risk among young people was commissioned (Goldston 2000). The review identifies instruments that have been used to evaluate suicidal behaviours in children and adolescents. Instruments are divided into those that assess:

1. the presence of suicidal behaviours

2. the risk or propensity for suicidal behaviours

3. the intentionality and medial lethality of suicidal behaviours

4. exposure to suicidal behaviour and other instruments.

Instruments that focus specifically on suicidal behaviours and those that focus on a wider range of behaviours are included in the review. Several methods were used in order to identify relevant instruments. Electronic database searches were conducted for the Social Science Citation Abstracts, PsycLiT (now PsycINFO) and Medline. In addition, the catalogues of major publishers of psychological tests were reviewed in order to identify new instruments. When reviewing instruments the definition of suicidal behaviours used and the psychometric characteristics (reliability and validity) of the instruments were discussed. Psychometric properties that were focused upon include: reliability, the extent to which a measurement tool produces similar results when repeated under similar conditions, internal consistency, the degree to which the components of the scale measure the same variables, concurrent validity, the degree to which scores on the scale correlate with those of other suicide risk assessment tools and predictive validity, the extent to which the scores on the test or scale are predictive of actual suicidal behaviour. There are a number of instruments that have been developed to assess risk or propensity for suicidal behaviour in children and adolescents. Some are well developed and their psychometric properties widely tested, others remain in the stages of development.

Beck Hopelessness Scale (BHS) (Beck et al. 1974b; Beck and Steer 1988; Steer and Beck 1988) USA

The Beck Hopelessness Scale (BHS) has come out of Beck's cognitive model of depression (Beck *et al.* 1979) in which hopelessness plays a prominent part. Hopelessness is also a common emotion experienced by suicidal patients (Shneidman 1996). The BHS includes 20 items and is designed to measure negative expectations about the future. Questions are answered based on the attitude of the person during the preceding week. It is therefore a self-report instrument and can be administered in written or oral form. Each of the items is scored with a true or false response. Total scores range from 0 to 20, with a higher score indicating a greater degree of hopelessness.

The BHS has been utilized with high school students (de Wilde *et al.*1993), adolescent psychiatric outpatients (Brent *et al.* 1997, 1998c), adolescent psychiatric inpatients (Enns *et al.*1997; Goldston *et al.* 2000; Kashden *et al.*1993) and adolescent suicide attempters on a paediatric unit (Swedo *et al.* 1991).

In terms of reliability and validity of the scale, hopelessness seems to be a relatively stable construct among psychiatrically hospitalized adolescents when assessed with the BHS (Goldston, unpublished data 2000. See also NIMH report at *www.nimh.nih.gov/suicideresearch/measures.pdf*). The scale has also been found to be internally consistent in adolescent psychiatric inpatients (Steer, Kumar and Beck 1993a). Hopelessness has been found to correlate with severity of depression (Enns *et al.*1997), suicidal ideation (Steer, Kumar and Beck 1993b) and repetition of suicidal behaviour (Goldston *et al.* 2000). BHS scores have been found to be predictive of suicide attempts following discharge from hospital among adolescent psychiatric inpatients with a history of suicide attempts, although these predictive effects were no longer significant once depression had been controlled for (Goldston *et al.* 2000). In another study, it was found that adolescents who dropped out of therapy had higher hopelessness scores than adolescents who remained in therapy (Brent *et al.* 1997).

The BHS has frequently been found to be associated with repeat suicide attempts and completed suicide among adults. It has also been found to predict later suicide attempts among psychiatrically hospitalized adolescents with a history of prior attempts, but not among young people without prior attempts.

Child Suicide Assessment (CSA) (Anderson and Larzelere 1997; Larzelere and Anderson 1998) USA

The development of the CSA was initiated owing to a lack of suitable screening instruments for assessing suicide risk in children between 6 and 12 years of age. The CSA is an interview-based instrument still in the stages of development. It is particularly relevant for adolescents under the age of 12, for whom most other suicide risk assessment instruments are not appropriate (Anderson and Larzelere 1997; Larzelere and Anderson 1998). The CSA is made up of three main sections focusing on 'feelings', 'family and friends' and 'child conception of death'. The answers to these questions are summed to produce an overall 'risk score'. The ranges of these scores associated with levels of risk are currently being developed. The CSA is currently being pilot tested on children. There are no published data available on reliability and validity of this scale.

Expendable Child Measure (Woznica and Shapiro 1990, 1998) USA

The Expendable Child Measure presents the interesting notion that young people who perceive themselves to be 'expendable' by their family members are at a greater risk of suicidal behaviour. That is, it assumes that suicidal youths perceive that their parents wish (consciously or unconsciously) to be rid of them or for them to die (Woznica and Shapiro 1990, 1998). It is a 12-item scale that is rated by the clinician. Items include 'patient feels like a burden on parent(s)/family', 'patient feels unwanted' etc. The scale helps to determine which adolescents need additional evaluation due to being at a particularly high risk for suicide. It can also be used to complement other measures of depression and suicidality.

The Expendable Child Measure has been used with adolescents in a hospital setting and outpatient clinic (Woznica and Shapiro 1998). There has been little published data on the psychometric characteristics of this measure, however it was found to be internally consistent with a sample of both suicidal and non-suicidal adolescent psychiatric outpatients (Woznica and Shapiro 1990). There has been no published data on reliability or predictive validity.

Firestone Assessment of Self-destructive Thoughts (FAST) (Firestone and Firestone 1998) USA

The FAST is a self-report instrument that is based on the theory associated with 'voice therapy' (Firestone and Firestone 1998). In this theory 'voices' are seen as internalized self-destructive negative thoughts that we gain from our parents. Self-destructive thoughts are divided into 11 levels associated with increasing suicidal ideation. Levels one to five indicate thoughts associated with low self-esteem and self-defeating tendencies, level six thoughts associated with addictions and levels seven to eleven thoughts associated with increasing risk of suicide. The FAST also contains a 'Suicidal Intent Composite', in order to differentiate individuals with and without suicidal ideation.

The FAST has been used with both clinical inpatient and outpatient samples. When tested in a sample of adolescent and (primarily) adult inpatients, the measure was found to have test-retest reliability. This was true for the entire FAST and for the Suicidal Intent Composite. The FAST has also been found to be internally consistent for a sample with both adolescents (age 16 and older) and adults. This was true for the entire FAST and for the Suicidal Intent Composite. Further, it has demonstrated concurrent validity, in that it correlates with the Suicide Probability Scale total score and the Beck Depression and Hopelessness Scales. There is no published data on the predictive validity of the scale however.

It is noteworthy however, that beyond the description of its development and validation, the FAST has not yet been used in published studies.

It was developed partly to measure suicidal potential, so the predictive validity of the scale needs to be examined.

Hopelessness Scale for Children (HPLS) (reproduced by Kazdin, Rodgers and Colbus 1986) USA

The HPLS is a modification of the Beck Hopelessness Scale (BHS) and is widely used in research studies into suicidality among young people. It is a 17-item scale and items are rated as either true or false with total scores ranging from 0 to 17. A higher score indicates a greater degree of hopelessness.

The HPLS was originally used with 6- to 13-year-old psychiatric inpatients (Kazdin et al. 1986), but has also been used with high school students (Cole 1989a; Reifman and Windle 1995), suicide attempters in a paediatric setting (Boergers, Spirito and Donaldson 1998; Spirito et al. 1987, 1988), child and adolescent psychiatric outpatients (Spirito et al. 1988) and with incarcerated adolescents (Cole 1989b).

The majority of studies using the HPLS have demonstrated the correlation of its scores with constructs related to depression and suicidal ideation or behaviour. Moderate stability has been obtained in HPLS scores among both child psychiatric inpatients (Kazdin et al. 1986) and among non-clinically referred adolescents (Spirito et al. 1988). The HPLS has been shown to be internally consistent with 6- to 13-year-old psychiatric inpatients (Kazdin et al. 1986), adolescent psychiatric inpatients (Hewitt et al. 1997). Further, concurrent validity has been demonstrated where HPLS scores were found to be correlated with a five-item questionnaire used by Beck et al. (1974b) to validate the Beck Hopelessness Scale (Cole 1989a). Higher HPLS scores were also found to be associated with a greater severity of depressive symptoms (Kazdin et al. 1986; Spirito et al. 1988), a higher prevalence of depressive diagnoses (Kashani et al. 1991) and poor self-esteem (Kashani et al. 1991; Kazdin et al. 1986). Mixed results have been obtained regarding whether HPLS scores are related to suicidality after depression has been controlled for.

In adults hopelessness has been found to be a predictor of future suicidal behaviour. However, research has failed to demonstrate the predictive validity of HPLS scores for the adolescent population. In a sample of 7- to 17-year-old inpatient and outpatient psychiatric patients HPLS scores were found not to be related to suicidality over a three-year follow-up period (Myers *et al.* 1991).

Inventory of Suicidal Orientation – 30 (ISO-30) (King and Kowalchuk 1994) USA

The ISO-30 (King and Kowalchuk 1994) is based on theory and has been described as a measure of 'life orientation' and of 'suicide risk'. It is designed to assess suicidality in 13- to 18-year-old adolescents. It is a 30-item self-report measure. It contains five scales related to hopelessness, suicidal ideation, perceived inadequacy, inability to cope with emotions and social isolation and withdrawal. Respondents are asked to respond based on how they have been thinking over the previous six months. Answers for each item are given using a four-point scale that ranges from 'I am sure I disagree' to 'I am sure I agree'. There are eight items that assess suicidal ideation and these are considered to be 'critical items'. The classification of risk of suicide (low, moderate or high) is based on a combination of the total scores obtained and the scores obtained on the critical items.

The ISO-30 has been tested in both clinically referred samples (King and Kowalchuk 1994; Piersma and Boes 1997) and in student samples (King and Kowalchuk 1994). When tested over a period of three to four days, it showed test-retest reliability overall and for the critical items (King and Kowalchuk 1994). The ISO-30 has also been found to be internally consistent when tested in adolescents from clinical and student samples (King and Kowalchuk 1994). ISO-30 scores have also been found to correlate with the SIQ and the SIQ-JR, which was also true for the critical items (King and Kowalchuk 1994).

Validation of this test has tended to focus on suicidal ideation only. Differences in test scores have not been demonstrated for both suicide attempters and non-suicide attempters, and the predictive validity of the instrument has been neglected.

Life Attitudes Schedule (LAS) (Lewinsohn *et al.* 1995) USA

The LAS is a self-report measure and is based on the theoretical notion that behaviour can be conceptualized on a continuum of life-enhancing and life-threatening behaviours. Half of the items on the LAS assess life-enhancing behaviours and half life-threatening behaviours. In addition, equal numbers of items assess thoughts, actions and feelings. A higher score on the LAS is thought to represent greater suicidal or self-destructive behaviour. Alternate forms of the LAS have also been developed (Lewinsohn *et al.* 1995) and a short form (Rohde *et al.* 1996).

The LAS has been used with high school students and with adolescents taking part in a treatment study for depression (Lewinsohn *et al.* 1995). Test-retest reliability has been established with high school students in a 30-day test-retest (Lewinsohn *et al.* 1995). Internal consistency of the alternate forms of the LAS has been established using a high school student sample (Lewinshon *et al.* 1995). The LAS is one of the only instruments for which issues of convergent validity and discriminant validity have been given attention. Items were selected in order to limit the degree of correlation with depression, hopelessness and social desirability in order to reduce the redundancy of items. No published data was located on the predictive validity of the scale.

Measure of Adolescent Potential for Suicide (MAPS) (Eggert, Thompson and Herting 1994) USA

The Suicide Risk Screen (SRS) and MAPS are used in a two-stage screening procedure to identify young people at high risk of suicidal behaviour. The first part of the assessment includes the High School Questionnaire within which are items relating to the SRS. This includes questions about current suicidal ideation and behaviours, depression and alcohol/drug use thought to be related to risk for suicidal behaviours. Part two of the assessment involves the MAPS interview (Eggert *et al.* 1994), which is face-to-face and computer assisted. The MAPS assesses direct suicide risk factors (exposure attitudes and belief about suicide), related risk factors (depression, hopelessness, anxiety, anger, school problems, alcohol/drug use etc.) and protective factors (self-esteem, personal control, coping strategies etc.).

The MAPS has been used to identify young people within the school system thought to be at risk for suicidal behaviour (Eggert *et al.* 1994; Thompson and Eggert 1999). Evidence for test-retest reliability of this measure is needed, however inter-rater reliability was established based on three videotaped MAPS interviews (Eggert *et al.* 1994). The internal consistency of the scales on the MAPS has been found to range from moderate to high (Eggert *et al.* 1994). The internal consistency of the SRS was also established to be high (Thompson and Eggert 1999). Most of the evidence regarding convergent and discriminative validity of the MAPS is provided by the relationships between the different scales of the MAPS. However, interviewer global ratings for each scale on the MAPS was found to correlate with ratings on the Los Angeles Suicide Potential Scale (Eggert *et al.* 1994). In the sense of predicting future suicidal behaviour, the predictive validity of the MAPS has not been examined.

Millon Adolescent Clinical Inventory (MACI) Suicidal Tendencies Scale (Millon 1993) USA

The MACI is designed to assess a number of personality constructs and psychological symptoms in adolescents. It is a 160- item self-report inventory to which respondents provide true or false answers. The MACI contains a scale on Suicidal Tendency.

The MACI Suicidal Tendency Scale has been used with adolescents who have been clinically referred (Hiatt and Cornell 1999; Millon 1993). Test-retest reliability was established in clinically referred samples of adolescents aged between 13 and 19 years of age (Millon 1993). Internal consistency was established in 13- to 19-year-old clinically referred samples (Millon 1993). Moderate to strong correlations have been found with scales assessing severity of depression, hopelessness, anxiety, social insecurity and problems with impulse regulation (Millon 1993). There is no published data on the predictive validity of the scale.

It is important to note that the evaluation of the psychometric properties of the scale does not go beyond the initial validation studies and the predictive validity of the scale is not known.

Multi-Attitude Suicide Tendency Scale (MAST) (Orbach *et al.* 1991) USA

The MAST is based on the idea that there is conflict among attitudes towards life and death. It is a 30-item measure assessing risk for suicidal behaviour. Attitudes that are assessed include attraction towards life, repulsion by life, attraction to death and repulsion by death.

The MAST has been used with samples of high school students, psychiatric outpatients and psychiatric inpatients (Orbach *et al.* 1991, 1999; Orbach, Lotem-Peleg and Kedem 1995). There is no published data on the reliability of the scale. Internal consistency however, was obtained for all four of the sub-scales of the MAST with high school students, inpatient and outpatient suicidal adolescents and non-suicidal psychiatric inpatients (Orbach *et al.* 1991). In clinical and non-clinical Israeli adolescents the four sub-scales of the MAST were found to correlate with the Israeli Index of Suicide Potential (Orbach *et al.* 1991). Attraction to death has also been found to be associated with suicidal ideation, suicide threats and the estimated likelihood of future suicide as assessed with the Suicide Probability Scale (Osman *et al.* 1994). Differences between suicidal and non-suicidal adolescents have also been observed (Orbach *et al.* 1991; Osman *et al.* 1994). There is no published data on the predictive validity of the scale.

PATHOS (Kingsbury 1996) UK

PATHOS aims to identify serious risk of adolescent overdose in those who are at a continued risk for suicidal behaviour. It is a five-item interview questionnaire that allows further assessment of patients prior to discharge from accident and emergency. The five items relate to five questions:

1. Have you had problems for longer than one month?

2. Were you alone in the house at the time?

3. Did you plan the overdose for longer than three hours?

4. Are you feeling hopeless about the future?

5. Were you feeling sad for most of the time before the overdose?

A score of two or greater for the five questions (yes counted as one) identified at-risk youths.

PATHOS has been used as a screening instrument in emergency settings for adolescents who present with overdose (Kingsbury 1996). No published data are available on the reliability of the measure and no published data have been located for internal consistency. PATHOS scores were found to be related, however, to independent assessments of depression, hopelessness, suicidal intent, premeditation time and history of prior overdose in a sample of adolescents presenting to an emergency room with overdoses (Kingsbury 1996). The utility of PATHOS in predicting later suicidal behaviour is unclear.

Reasons for Living (RFL) (Linehan et al. 1983) USA

The RFL questionnaire assesses belief systems that 'buffer' against suicidal behaviour. That is, it assesses potential reasons for not committing suicide. It is a self-report measure, from which different versions have been produced. The most commonly used contains 48 items. Items are rated on their importance as a reason for suicide. Items are scored on a six-point Likert scale that range from 'not at all important' to 'extremely important'. In this way, the RFL assesses:

1.   survival and coping beliefs

2.   responsibility to family

3.   child-related concerns

4.   fear of suicide

5.   fear of social disapproval

6.   moral objections.

A total score is obtained as well as a score for each of the above. Other versions of the RFL include the Brief Reasons for Living (BRFL, Ivanoff et al. 1994), the Brief RFL for Adolescents (BRFL-A, Osman et al. 1998) and the Brief RFL for adolescents (BRFL-A, Osman et al. 1996).

The RFL has been used with incarcerated adolescents, student populations (Cole 1989b) and with adolescent psychiatric inpatients (Goldston et al. 2000; Pinto, Whisman and Conwell 1998). No published data were located on the reliability of the measure. However, the RFL has been found to be internally consistent with psychiatric inpatients (Pinto et al. 1998). Survival and coping beliefs and responsibility to family scales of the RFL have been found to be negatively related to suicidal ideation, past suicide threats, past suicide attempts, estimated likelihood of future attempts, severity of depression and hopelessness in samples of high school students and incarcerated youths (Cole 1989b). Not all of the scales within the RFL seem to have equal utility in predicting suicidal behaviour. The survival and coping beliefs scales of the RFL for inpatient adolescents with a history of suicide attempts have the most items, highest levels of internal consistency, convergent validity and are alone among the RFL scales in having some predictive validity with adolescents (Goldston *et al.* 2000).

Reasons for Living – Adolescent (RFL-A) (Osman *et al.* 1998) USA and Brief Reasons for Living – Adolescent (BRFL-A) (Osman *et al.* 1996) USA

These two instruments were developed from the RFL inventory and are thought to assess the same life-maintaining belief system as the RFL. The RFL-A contains 52 items and the BRFL-A 14 items.

Non-clinical high school students and adolescent psychiatric inpatients have been used as validation populations for the RFL-A and the BRFL-A (Osman *et al.* 1996, 1998). No published data were located on the reliability of the scales. The BRFL-A has been found to be internally consistent in a sample of high school students and adolescent psychiatric inpatients (Osman *et al.* 1996). Internal consistency was also shown for the RFL-A in non-clinical high school students and adolescent psychiatric inpatients (Gutierrez *et al.* 2000; Osman *et al.* 1998). The survival and coping beliefs and responsibility to family scales of the BRFL-A were found to correlate negatively with current suicidal ideation, self-rated expectation of later suicide attempts and estimated suicide probability (Osman *et al.* 1996). Also the RFL-A total and scale scores have been found to be moderately negatively correlated with suicide ideation, suicide threats and estimated likelihood of future attempts as assessed by the Suicide Behaviour Questionnaire, the Suicide Probability Scale, the Beck Hopelessness Scale and the depression section of the Brief Symptom Inventory (Osman *et al.* 1998). No published data were located on the predictive validity of the scales.

It appears that both the RFL-A and the BRFL-A may have greater utility with adolescent populations than the original RFL. However, research to date is limited to validation studies, with no documentation of the predictive validity of the scales.

Suicide Probability Scale (SPS) (Cull and Gill 1988) USA

The SPS acts as a screening instrument for the identification of at-risk adolescents aged 14 or older (Cull and Gill 1988). It is a 36-item self-report measure. The items of the SPS assess hopelessness, suicidal ideation, negative self-evaluation and hostility. Respondents are asked to indicate whether each item describes them on a scale ranging from 'none or a little of the time' to 'most or all of the time'. The SPS has a total score and a total score for each of the sub-scales (pertaining to the areas described above). The manual of the SPS presents no evidence about the predictive utility of the scale.

The primary validation of the SPS was using an adult sample (Cull and Gill 1988) and evidence is mixed as to the utility of the scale in the adolescent population. It has also been used with high school students (D'Attilio et al. 1992; Tatman, Greene and Karr 1993), paediatric health clinic attendees (Cappelli et al. 1995), physically abused young people (Kaplan et al. 1997), adolescents in a group home setting (Larzelere et al. 1996) and adolescent psychiatric inpatients (Osman et al. 1996). Test-retest reliability and internal consistency have been established for the SPS (Cull and Gill 1988). The total SPS score was found to be negatively correlated with the survival and coping beliefs, responsibility to family and moral objections scales and the total score of the BRFL-A in a sample of adolescent psychiatric inpatients (Osman et al. 1996). SPS scores have also been found to be negatively associated with the total RFL-A score and all of the RFL-A scales (Osman et al. 1998). Further, SPS scores were found to be predictive of future suicidal behaviour in a sample of adolescents receiving treatment in a group home (Larzelere et al. 1996). There were, however, questions about the 'cut-off' score recommended in the SPS manual being too low.

Zung Index of Potential Suicide (IPS) (Zung 1974) USA

The IPS was developed 25 years ago primarily for the screening of adults. The IPS is divided into two parts. One of which is comprised of social and demographic variables associated with risk (previous hospitalizations, recent moves, recent losses, religion etc.) and the other clinical variables (depressed mood, symptoms of depression, symptoms of anxiety, substance abuse, aggression, hopelessness etc.). The second part of the IPS is further divided into three components: a form completed by an interviewer (rated from 0, 'none, not present or insignificant' to 4, 'severe in intensity or duration, present most or all of the time in frequency'), a self-rating form (rated from 0, 'none of the time' to 4, 'most or all of the time') and a form completed by a significant other. The IPS was primarily developed for use with adults and some of the socio-demographic variables are therefore not appropriate.

The IPS has been mainly used with non-clinical adolescent populations (Cole 1989a, 1989b). No published test-retest reliability data or data in relation to internal consistency were located for adolescent samples. For concurrent validity, questions extracted from the IPS regarding suicidal ideation, suicide plans and suicide attempts were found to be moderately negatively correlated with the survival and coping beliefs scale of the RFL in a sample of high school students (Cole 1989b). No published data on the predictive validity of the scale were located.

Summary points

A number of screening instruments for the identification of at-risk adolescents exist, the majority of which have been developed in the USA.

A review of the existing screening instruments utilized for identifying adolescents who are at risk from suicidal behaviour highlights the following:

- More prospective studies are needed in order to investigate the predictive validity of assessment instruments.

- More attention needs to be paid to discriminate validity, i.e. the degree to which suicidal behaviour does not correlate with constructs that it should not.

- Attention needs to be given to that fact that different risk assessment instruments will have different utility in differing populations.

Despite these points, there has been a large growth in interest within the last ten years in the assessment of young people thought to be at risk of suicidality. It does appear, however, that more attention has been given to the development of new instruments rather than the evaluation of the utility of existing tools (Goldston 2000).

When discussing screening instruments for the identification of at-risk individuals, it is important to include a cautionary note. In clinical work with adolescents, owing to them possessing little power, they can have a useful adjunctive role but should not be used as the sole or primary means of assessing risk.

5 Services for Adolescents

Commissioning services

Young people who deliberately self-harm require a range of agencies and sectors of care. For example, initial physical and mental health care may fall on the health service, with a full and longer-term approach provided through the co-ordination of both local and health authorities and non-statutory sector agencies.

It is therefore important that statutory sector authorities ensure that

> the needs of young people who harm themselves are fully included in the children's services plans that each local authority is required to prepare in consultation with the relevant health authorities. (Royal College of Psychiatrists 1998, p.5)

Furthermore, within the overall plans for child and adolescent mental health services, health authorities/boards should identify the resources needed for the appropriate assessment and treatment of young deliberate self-harmers. The required resources should be based on local assessments of need, not neglecting the national position. It is important that each health authority/board works with relevant NHS trusts in order to clarify immediate and long-term physical and mental health care with respect to assessment, admission and continuing care. Commissioners also need to ensure appropriate expertise and services are available for young people with psychiatric disorders and learning disabilities.

Some young people will require emergency psychiatric care after deliberate self-harm and may require admission to a psychiatric inpatient unit with specialist resources. In these cases, health authorities need to estimate the number of specialized admissions needed each year and commission services prospectively, including the allocation of budgets within their plans for child and adolescent mental health services. Locally the way that units are arranged may be complex. As a result, the council report produced by the Royal College of Psychiatrists (1998) puts forward a number of points in order to facilitate this process.

Each health authority/board should:

(i)   work with partner local authorities, trusts and primary care groups/teams to ensure that inter-agency boundaries do not create fault lines in service delivery;

(ii) ensure that it has service agreements or contracts with the necessary range of provider agencies within its area of responsibility;

(iii) ensure that the range of provider agencies has service agreements between them that enable protocols for assessing and treating young people who harm themselves to be put in place and used effectively.

(Royal College of Psychiatrists 1998, p.6)

The significance of deliberate self-harm in young people should also be recognized in the health improvement programmes of health authorities and boards. Improvement programmes should focus on the requirements of service providers to plan and negotiate adequate local services, in order to provide a comprehensive, immediate and longer-term intervention for young people who deliberately self-harm.

A useful text when commissioning services for adolescents has been put forward by Williams and Morgan (1994). Entitled *Suicide Prevention: The Challenge Confronted,* it provides advice to health authorities/boards, including a checklist for evaluating plans and the quality of services that they commission for adolescents who deliberately harm themselves.

Delivering services

Local protocols

It is important that professional staff and managers agree with protocols. This will be true for professionals from child and adolescent mental health, accident and emergency, paediatrics and child health, including those who provide general medical services, substance misuse services and learning disability services. This will mean that service agreements need to be made between trusts and across relevant clinical directorates. The Council Report of the Royal College of Psychiatrists (1998) recommends that a consultant paediatrician and a consultant adolescent psychiatrist be joint service leaders due to the complementary aspect of the care that these two professionals provide for young people who deliberately harm themselves.

Hospital admission

Initially, emergency physical assessment and treatment will be needed. This should also be accompanied by an initial assessment of the patient's mental state, usually in an accident and emergency department. After this stage of acute presentation, it is usually desirable that the young person be admitted to a paediatric, adolescent or medical ward, or to a designated unit, although it is generally recommended that admissions should be to a paediatric ward. Policy and practice for the arrangement of admissions need to be agreed locally by those responsible.

During admission, the young person should remain in the overall care of a paediatrician.

Assessment and treatment

It is important to assess suicidal ideation and the risk of acting on suicidal or self-harming impulses, and to make a preliminary assessment of the overall mental health and development of the young person, including their psychosocial situation and the ability of responsible adults to ensure their safety. Due to the anxiety that deliberate self-harm can cause, it is recommended that professionals who work within specialist child and adolescent mental health services carry out the processes of assessment and management planning.

As a result of the demands of such work, it is important that these professionals are trained specifically to work with young people and their families after deliberate self-harm, that they be skilled in risk assessment and have consultation and supervision available to them.

Williams and Morgan (1994) have put forward a protocol for the assessment of children and adolescents, which includes assessing risk of deliberate self-harm in adolescents.

Summary points

Young people who engage in self-harming behaviour require a range of agencies and sectors of care. They come into contact with a large number of different professionals. These include doctors and nurses in accident and emergency departments, psychiatrists, paediatricians and psychologists. As such, when delivering services for adolescents who deliberately self-harm, interdisciplinary liaison and co-operation is essential for good clinical practice. It is important that general hospital and aftercare services are delivered according to recommended standards.

When commissioning services for deliberate self-harmers, it is important to identify the relevant resources based on local assessments of need, not neglecting the national position. Immediate and long-term physical and mental health care with respect to assessment, admission and continuing care all need to be catered for.

6 The Outcome of Suicidal Behaviour in Adolescence

Child to adult follow-up

The long-term outcome for children and adolescents who engage in non-fatal deliberate self-harm is unclear.

Research that has been carried out in the United Kingdom has found an increased risk of completed suicide following attempted suicide. Studies of adult samples investigating the rate of suicide following deliberate self-harm over the longer term have yielded figures of 3% within an eight-year period following an episode (Hawton and Fagg 1988) and 7% with follow-up at longer than ten years (De Moore and Robertson 1996). However, Otto (1972) found a lower figure in a study in which adolescent suicide attempters were followed up for 10 to 15 years following an episode. He found that suicide had occurred in 4.3% of individuals in the adolescent sample. Other studies following up adolescent self-poisoners have found average annual death rates of nearly four times the average rates found in the national population as a whole in this age group (Goldacre and Hawton 1985). Similarly, Sellar *et al.* (1990) followed up adolescent self-poisoners (mean 3.6 years) and found that the average annual death rates were 0.6 per 1000 females and 2.8 per 1000 males. The figure obtained for males was significantly higher than the corresponding rate (0.8 per 1000) for the general population of males of a similar age. Suicidal inpatients are at a substantial risk for making a repeat attempt within six months of discharge. Brent *et al.* (1993a) followed up adolescent inpatients who were admitted for a suicide attempt or suicidal ideation and found that 9.7% had made a suicide attempt within six months.

From a retrospective viewpoint utilizing psychological autopsy studies, it has been found in one study that about half of all people who commit suicide have a history of deliberate self-harm. In 20 to 25% of cases an episode of deliberate self-harm will have occurred within the last year (Hawton *et al.* 1998). A number of factors have been associated with a higher risk of later suicide in adolescents who deliberately self-harm. These include: male gender, older age, high suicidal intent, psychosis, depression, hopelessness and not having a clear reason for the act of deliberate self-harm (Royal College of Psychiatrists 1998). Greater disturbance at the time of initial contact and psychiatric hospitalization are also thought to increase this risk (Shaffer and Piacentini 1994).

Repetition rates of deliberate self-harm that have been put forward are between 6% and 30% (NHS Centre for Reviews and Dissemination 1998). The wide variation is thought to be due to differences in sample selection and in different rates in different locations. A systematic review carried out by Owens, Horrocks and House (2002) investigated rates of fatal and non-fatal repetition of self-harm. One year later 16% of patients had repeated acts of non-fatal self-harm, with 2% having been fatal. Seven per cent of patients had died by suicide after more than nine years. Other studies have found that repetition usually occurs not long after an episode of deliberate self-harm, reporting a median time of 72 days for those with a history of self-harm (Gilbody, House and Owens 1997; Wilkinson and Smeeton 1987).

Repetition rates for adolescent self-poisoning have been reported to be as high as 10%, although most studies have suffered from small sample sizes (Haldane and Haider 1967; Hawton *et al.* 1982a). Goldacre and Hawton (1985) followed up adolescent self-poisoners for a mean period of 2.8 years and found that 6.3% had repeated within one year. Two reported episodes were recorded in 6.6% of patients, 1.7% of patients had three recorded episodes, 0.9% had four and 0.3% had five or more during the follow-up period. Death rates were found to be four times higher than the national average annual death rates found in the general population in this age group. A further study undertaken by Sellar *et al.* (1990) provided updated information to the Goldacre and Hawton (1985) study. They followed up adolescent self-poisoners for a mean period of 3.6 years and found that 6.6% had been further admitted to hospital within one year. Rates of repetition were found to be higher for females at 10.5% than for males (9.3%). Repetition rates were also higher among the 16 to 20 age range than among 12- to 15-year-olds. Overall, 10.2% of self-poisoners had repeat episodes within the mean 3.6 years follow-up time.

Experiencing personality disturbance later on in life such as repeated separations, poor social problem-solving and impaired peer relationships have been reported as risk factors for children and adolescents who have harmed themselves (Andrews and Lewinsohn 1992; Kerfoot et al. 1996; Sadowski and Kelly 1993).

One study that investigated factors associated with suicide after deliberate self-harm in young people was carried out by Hawton et al. (1993). The study was of a case-control design, with 62 cases (41 suicides and 21 possible suicides) and 124 controls aged between 15 and 24 years. It aimed to investigate possible predictors of completed suicide. Findings indicated that suicide and possible suicide was associated with social class V, unemployment, previous inpatient psychiatric treatment, substance misuse, personality disorder and previous attempted suicide. The critical appraisal of the paper highlighted that although data on deaths were available from the Register General's Office in Scotland, cases were identified from a single hospital, which may bias results owing to the way in which that particular hospital recorded data; that is whether it was recorded in a reliable way. Information that was obtained was not based on human recall, controlling for this type of bias. The controls who were used in the study were selected from the same population as cases, and seemed only to differ in whether they had died or not.

Overall, 28 variables were assessed, including socio-demographic variables, background, psychiatric variables, previous parasuicide episodes and method of parasuicide. Participants were matched by sex and age. Cases were selected from a single hospital, which needs to be kept in mind when generalizing results to other populations because the results found may be owing to factors associated with that particular hospital. Other limitations of the study (which the authors acknowledge) include that deaths from suicide were only obtained for subjects living in Edinburgh at the time of death; subjects who had moved away were not taken account of and this may have led to bias. In order to avoid this bias, a cohort that had been followed up completely would be necessary. Nevertheless, results are in line with previous work that suggests that adolescents who engage in suicidal behaviour are at a greater risk for eventual suicide.

More research is needed in order to clarify the risk factors of deliberate self-harm in later life. Research also needs to adopt a more robust methodology enabling follow-up into adulthood of children and adolescents who engage in acts of non-fatal deliberate self-harm.

Summary points

The future outlook for children and adolescents who engage in non-fatal self-harming behaviour is unclear. There is some suggestion that there is an increased risk of suicide and an increased risk of repetition of deliberate self-harm, following an act of deliberate self-harm. A small body of research cites an increased risk of later personality disturbance such as repeated separations, poor social problem-solving and impaired peer relationships. However, very little research has been conducted that specifically follows up children and adolescents who exhibit suicidal behaviour into adulthood, limiting conclusions that can be made.

7 Managing Adolescent Suicidal Behaviour

It helps a lot when I can be with someone I trust. I need people to understand me, support me. I need to be treated normally – just like anyone else. Not like a mad person. I'm not mad. I've just got problems because of what happened in my past. Something happens – and suddenly all the memories and feelings come back.

(YoungMinds 2003, p.10)

Immediate and general hospital management

The majority of patients who receive treatment following deliberate self-harm will first have presented to a general hospital with deliberate self-poisoning or self-injury. Immediate assessment of the medical consequences of the self-poisoning or self-injury is needed as well as a brief assessment of the patient's psychiatric status and risk. It is particularly important to determine whether the patient has a serious psychiatric disorder, for example psychosis or severe depression, and is actively suicidal. Potential methods of self-harm should be removed and staff should be aware of the possibility that the patient might leave before the psychiatric assessment has been conducted.

The psychiatric assessment of patients should only take place once the adolescent has recovered from the neurotoxic effects of an attempt. However, if the patient is severely disturbed or at acute risk then a more urgent assessment should take place. The assessment should take the form of a semi-structured interview with the use of questionnaires. Factors that should be covered include:

1. preceding life events

2. motives, including suicidal intent

3. problems that the patient has faced

4. psychiatric illness

5. personality traits and disorder

6. alcohol and drug misuse

7. family and personal history

8. current circumstances

9. psychiatric history, including previous attempts

10. risk of further deliberate self-harm

11. risk of completed suicide

12. coping resources and support

13. appropriate treatment

14. motivation to engage in treatment.

When assessing the patient's problems and events that preceded the act of deliberate self-harm, it is useful to obtain a very detailed account of the few days before the attempt. This information should be supplemented by obtaining information from other sources such as relatives or friends, including professionals involved in the patient's care, such as their general practitioner.

Suicidal intent can be assessed using a range of instruments (see Chapter Four, section on screening instruments for the identification of at-risk individuals). Probably the best established instrument is the Beck Suicidal Intent Scale (Beck, Schuyler and Herman 1974a), which assesses factors such as whether the act was carried out in isolation, whether precautions were taken to avoid discovery or the person had made preparations in the anticipation of their death.

Motivational reasons for deliberate self-harm are usually assessed in terms of precedents, circumstances surrounding the act and information given by the patient and others. A useful list of reasons has been developed based on research conducted in the 1970s (Bancroft *et al.* 1977; Birtchnell and Alarcon 1971; Hawton *et al.* 1982b).

Box 7.1 Motives or reasons for deliberate self-harm

- To die.
- To escape from unbearable anguish.
- To get relief.
- To escape from a situation.
- To show desperation to others.
- To change the behaviour of others.
- To get back at other people/make them feel guilty.
- To get help.

(Hawton and van Heeringen 2000, p.523)

It is also important to estimate the risk of repetition of deliberate self-harm, focusing on previous attempts, psychiatric history, whether the person has a personality disorder or is abusing alcohol and drugs for example. Risk of suicide should also be considered. Similar factors are relevant, with substance misuse being especially important (Hawton *et al.* 1993). Coping resources and support can be assessed on past behaviour when under stress and the patient's account of who they can turn to for help and support.

An important question that arises in general hospital management is who should assess patients who deliberately self-harm? In the 1960s in the United Kingdom, official guidelines specified that all deliberate self-harm patients should be assessed by psychiatrists (Ministry of Health

1961). It was seen therefore that deliberate self-harm patients were primarily the responsibility of psychiatry. Subsequently, however, it was shown that social workers, nurses and other clinicians can reliably assess patients who deliberately self-harm and make effective aftercare arrangements and in addition, provide effective therapy (Catalan *et al.* 1980; Gardner *et al.* 1978; Hawton *et al.* 1981; Newson-Smith and Hirsch 1979). As a result, new official guidelines were issued (Department of Health and Social Security 1984; Royal College of Psychiatrists 1994).

Staff who are involved in the assessment and treatment of patients who deliberately self-harm need to be properly trained and have experience and skills in the management of patients with emotional and psychiatric disorders. Support from senior psychiatrists is also very important, especially where patients have severe psychiatric disorders or have been compulsorily admitted to hospital.

Another issue that arises in the general hospital management of patients who deliberately self-harm is that of compliance with treatment. Those who attempt suicide are notoriously bad at complying with treatment, and this poses a problem for those who are administering treatment. Trautman, Stewart and Morishima (1993) investigated whether adolescent suicide attempters were non-compliant with outpatient care, through studying attendance at an outpatient clinic. They reported a 77% drop out rate. This occurred quite quickly with a median number of three visits before drop out. Patients who discharge themselves from accident and emergency before completion of initial assessment have been found to be three times more likely to repeat self-harm compared to those who received assessment by a psychiatrist or specialist nurse before discharge (Crawford and Wessely 1998).

Aftercare

Although adolescents make up a significant proportion of those who attempt suicide, few intervention studies have specifically investigated this age group. Studies that have been conducted have more often utilized all-age or adult populations. Findings of these studies however may not be directly generalizable to adolescents. First, the outcome for adolescents who attempt suicide is different from older suicide attempters, that is to say adolescent suicide attempts have a lower rate of subsequent completed suicide in the short to medium term (Safer 1997a). Second, treatment strategies that have been shown to be effective in adult populations may not necessarily elicit the same response in adolescents (Hazell *et al.* 1995).

Once an adolescent has received a mental health assessment in an emergency department, he or she will be discharged to the care of their parents or guardians or to the care of the welfare agencies. An appointment is usually arranged in an outpatient or community clinic in order to provide follow-up for the adolescent, although treatment non-adherence is common. Typically, suicidal adolescents receive a period of intensive intervention following a suicide attempt, followed by intermittent low-intensity contact.

Psychotherapeutic approaches to treatment

There is no consensus regarding the best therapeutic intervention although a substantial amount of literature on various forms of psychotherapeutic interventions for suicidal patients exists. However, the research lacks robust methodology, particularly in relation to a controlled treatment design. Despite this, psychotherapy is widely used in the treatment of suicidal individuals. Therapies that have been evaluated in controlled trials include cognitive-behavioural therapies such as problem-solving therapy and cognitive therapy, and outreach and intensive therapies. A number of other treatments may also be utilized such as social skills training, recognition and regulation of anger and family therapy.

PROBLEM-SOLVING THERAPY

Problem-solving therapy hypothesizes that suicidal behaviour is due to an individual having a lack of psychological resources to resolve their problem in any other way. Patients are encouraged to play a very active role in identifying and understanding their problems and are encouraged to generate and implement adaptive solutions. First, the therapist will help the patient to define the problems and to identify factors that contribute to them. In order to understand these factors, it may be useful to identify events, thoughts, emotions and behaviours leading up to a recent maladaptive behaviour.

The therapist will then help the patient to generate solutions to the problem identified. The solutions will then be evaluated and the chosen solutions implemented. Possible solutions are generated through brainstorming – generating as many solutions as possible, however odd or extreme. Evaluation of the solutions produced will comprise a discussion of their pros and cons. However, suicidal patients tend to focus on the potential negative outcomes of alternative solutions. In order to overcome this bias the therapist might therefore teach the patient new skills, challenge the patient's style of thinking and their thoughts, and help the patient gain rewards for implementing solutions. The therapist will 'coach' the patient in implementing solutions by helping the patient to rehearse the solutions both cognitively and behaviourally. This will enable the identification of any problems that might hinder the implementation of any solutions.

One non-randomized clinical trial carried out by Donaldson *et al.* (1997) looked at adolescents who were administered problem-solving therapy via the telephone and compared them with subjects receiving standard aftercare. They found fewer repeat attempts in the problem-solving group. However, this result was not statistically significant. Four other randomized controlled trials in older patients have also shown a trend in favour of problem-solving therapy over standard aftercare, although the trend was again not statistically significant (Hawton *et al.* 1998). Benefits of problem-solving therapy have been shown, however, for improvement in depression, hopelessness and problem-solving (Salkovskis, Atha and Storer 1990; Townsend *et al.* 2001).

COGNITIVE-BEHAVIOUR THERAPY

Cognitive-behaviour therapy used to treat suicidal behaviour is primarily derived from the cognitive therapies that were developed to treat depression. Cognitive-behaviour therapy postulates that the way that individuals interpret events and experiences affects how they feel and behave. Individuals develop automatic patterns of thinking which are distortions of reality. This in turn activates maladaptive coping behaviours such as suicidal behaviour. The cognitive distortions that a person has developed will also be maintained by the basic underlying assumptions that they have about themselves, the world and the future.

The cognitive-behaviour therapist therefore aims to change the individual's cognitive content and processes in order to change their suicidal behaviour and associated affect. The actual cognitive techniques used are similar to those used in problem-solving therapy; however cognitive therapy may also include behavioural techniques.

OUTREACH AND INTENSIVE THERAPIES

Outreach and intensive therapies include psychotherapy programmes that add outreach components, or intensify standard outpatient treatment. These therapies employ a variety of treatment interventions. Increasing the intensity of treatment may involve increasing the duration or frequency of therapy sessions or adding extra modalities; for example, individual therapy plus family therapy. Outreach may be provided by telephone, letter or home visit.

SOCIAL SKILLS TRAINING

Social skills training teaches more effective communication with people with whom the adolescent has disagreement. This is often done through role-play. It can also be used to encourage assertiveness and to improve confidence in social situations.

RECOGNITION AND REGULATION OF ANGER

The purpose of recognition and regulation of anger is to identify and control feelings of anger before they escalate to suicidal behaviour. Both the adolescent and their family members are taught how to recognize signs of increasing tension. When the adolescent reaches the 'point of no return' is also discussed, where there is likely to be some disruptive behaviour. In order to do this, what is called a 'feeling thermometer' is used, on which these points can be mapped. Once the signs of increasing tension and 'the point of no return' have been identified and mapped onto the 'feeling thermometer', strategies for dealing with feelings of anger can then be identified and employed where appropriate (Rotheram 1987): for example, temporary disengagement in order to defuse a difficult situation.

FAMILY THERAPY

Family therapies can vary with some adopting a family psycho-educational approach, while others focus more on conflict resolution and communication skills.

One randomized controlled trial carried out by Harrington *et al.* (1998) focused exclusively on the adolescent population. They randomly allocated consecutive cases of deliberate self-poisoning admitted to four hospitals in Manchester. All adolescents were under the age of 17 years, with 77 allocated routine care and 85 to routine care plus brief family intervention. The family intervention consisted of an assessment followed by four home visits that focused on family communication and problem-solving. Both groups were assessed at time of recruitment and at a two and a six-month follow-up. Outcome measures included: Suicidal Ideation Questionnaire (Reynolds 1988), the Family Assessment Device (Miller *et al.* 1985), the General Health Questionnaire (Goldberg 1978) and the Deliberate Self-Harm Interview Schedule (Kerfoot 1988). No significant differences were found between the two groups for any of the outcome measures at any of the assessment times. That is, there was no beneficial effect of intensive intervention with home visiting compared with standard aftercare. The authors conclude that brief forms of intervention are only likely to be effective in subjects without major depression, who tend to show less severe forms of suicidal behaviour. Studies looking at more intensive forms of family intervention are needed in order to determine whether they are more effective in leading to better outcomes for adolescents (Harrington *et al.* 2000).

Experimental treatment

A number of novel treatment strategies have been investigated. For example, home visiting, emergency green cards and emergency department programmes. One randomized controlled trial (Harrington *et al.* 1998) and one non-randomized clinical trial (Deykin *et al.* 1986) looked at the efficacy of an intensive intervention with home visiting compared to standard aftercare for adolescent suicide attempters. No benefit of the intensive intervention was found. This was consistent with data obtained for adult samples (Hawton *et al.* 1998), although in these samples home visiting has been found to improve other aspects of functioning. Another study, a randomized controlled trial, investigated the use of an emergency green card (Cotgrove *et al.* 1995). In this study the emergency card provided the suicide attempter with 24-hour access to clinical follow-up. This experimental group was compared to a group of subjects given standard aftercare. Eleven per cent of the experimental group made use of their green card to gain access to hospital. Six per cent of the experimental group made further suicide attempts in the following year compared to 12 per cent of the control group. Although a trend towards a reduction in repetition with the use of the green card was observed, this did not reach statistical significance. Morgan, Jones and Owen (1993), however, investigated the effect of a green card on the repetition of deliberate self-harm and found that the experimental group showed a significant reduction in actual or seriously threatened deliberate self-harm. This group also made less demands on medical and psychiatric services compared to the control group. It is important to note that the mean age of subjects, however, was 30 years. Another experimental treatment that has been investigated was a programme introduced to a hospital emergency department (Rotheram-Borus *et al.* 1996). It consisted of staff education, a psycho-educational video for adolescent suicide attempters and their families emphasizing the importance of follow-up and an emergency family therapy session. Both the experimental group and the control group were then offered standard aftercare. Repetition rates were not reported. However, the experimental group reported lower depression and suicidal ideation at follow-up. No significant difference in adherence to aftercare was found between the two groups.

It is important to note that novel treatment strategies are often measured against 'standard aftercare'. This is owing to ethical concerns having been raised about assigning patients at risk for suicidal behaviour, a high-risk population, to a control or comparison group that may be less effective than standard treatment. In fact, standard aftercare is often not supported by empirical evidence but developed through clinical expertise and adopted by consensus. There is also considerable heterogeneity in the standard aftercare that adolescent suicide attempters receive. Spirito *et al.* (2002) carried out a study of treatment-as-usual (TAU) in a sample of 63 adolescent suicide attempters. They found that following a suicide attempt the adolescents attended between 0 and 22 outpatient psychotherapy sessions, with a mean of seven sessions. Fifty-two per cent of the adolescents reported having attended six or fewer sessions. Three quarters of the sample had received supportive psychotherapy; half had received psychodynamic and cognitive therapy and a third behavioural therapy. This type of treatment therefore does not lend itself to systematic evaluation. The aftercare that is received will depend more on factors such as the availability of treatment resources and financing of the medical services of the area. For example, in the USA adolescents are three times more likely to receive psychiatric hospitalization following a suicide attempt than adolescents in Western Europe (Safer 1996). They are also offered up to four times as many outpatient follow-up visits as adolescents in the United Kingdom (Brent 1997).

The efficacy of aftercare and its outcome

There is little consensus as to the type of aftercare needed for individuals who present with deliberate self-harm and do not require inpatient or other residential services. As a result, the treatment that is available tends to vary greatly across the country. A sizeable literature can be found that proposes models of intervention and methods of aftercare (Allard, Marshall and Plante 1992; Deykin *et al.* 1986; Shaffer *et al.* 1988; Tolan, Ryan and Jaffe 1988). However, within this literature there are very few controlled studies that investigate interventions within the adolescent population within the United Kingdom (or indeed elsewhere). It is important to have well-defined studies that focus on the efficacy of after-care and its outcome because episodes of deliberate self-harm are often markers of severe interpersonal, social or even psychiatric problems such as behavioural problems or depression. Well-defined studies investigating the long-term outcome of deliberate self-harm are therefore much needed.

Research that has investigated the characteristics of young people with suicidal behaviour in the United Kingdom has highlighted important factors that might be useful and relevant when designing and providing interventions (Hawton *et al.* 1982a, 1982b; Kerfoot 1988; Taylor and Stansfield 1984a, 1984b). Young people who engage in suicidal behaviour tend to come from families with disturbed relationships and high interpersonal and social stress. Communication is often poor

(Richman 1979) and their ability to solve problems limited (Hawton 1986). Interventions therefore need to be targeted at both individual and family functioning. Young people are also often difficult to engage in treatment and to follow-up (Taylor and Stansfield 1984a, 1984b). This is not surprising, given that suicidal behaviour is a highly emotive issue and feelings of guilt, blame and embarrassment are often prominent. Families may deny the seriousness of what has happened and view therapeutic intervention as an unwelcome and painful reminder of the suicidal episode.

Research suggests that treatments that are actively engaging and challenging for the individual, and have flexibility in terms of time and locational setting (Kerfoot 1996) are likely to be more successful than traditional approaches. Research has also indicated that treatment approaches that address specific difficulties such as negative cognitions, poor problem-solving and dysfunctional family communication are likely to be more successful in reducing suicidal ideation and increasing treatment compliance.

Van der Sande et al. (1997) and Hawton et al. (1998, 2001) have carried out systematic reviews of the literature related to the efficacy of psychosocial and pharmacological treatment interventions in reducing the repetition of deliberate self-harm.

Van der Sande et al. (1997) identified 31 papers in their review. Psychosocial treatment and prospective randomized trials of interventions aimed at improving compliance with aftercare were included whose primary outcome measured was repeated suicide attempts. Randomized controlled trials that were identified were divided into those that focused on the psychiatric management of poor compliance, psychosocial intervention, guaranteed inpatient shelter in an emergency and cognitive-behavioural therapies. The critical appraisal of this study revealed that although the question states that it is a systematic review of prospective randomized controlled trials on secondary prevention programmes for repeated suicide attempters, there is no description of the population, for example, age range to be included. Psychosocial/psychotherapeutic treatments only are included and the outcome measured is repeated suicide attempts.

The literature search involved Medline (1966 onwards) and PsycLIT (now PsycINFO, 1974 onwards). The references of identified papers were also hand searched. There was no mention of whether any grey literature was searched, thus it seems reasonable to assume that this was neglected. Publication bias may therefore be an issue. Inclusion criteria seem clear and appropriate, however, and the authors incorporated certain exclusion criteria. The overall effect size was measured using an overall relative risk estimate ($RR_{overall}$). No effect for psychiatric management of poor compliance/availability of inpatient shelter/psychosocial interventions was found. An effect for cognitive-behavioural therapy was found, however, with 50% of individuals prevented from carrying out a repeat attempt.

Results were fairly consistent from study to study in each of the groups. Intervention type varied, so the authors grouped the interventions into four categories. Results were clearly displayed. It seems reasonable to have combined the results. A Chi-square statistic revealed no significant heterogeneity. Conclusions do seem to flow from the evidence that was presented and sub-group analyses that were carried out are interpreted with caution. In terms of generalizability of results, the significant effect of cognitive-behavioural therapy on reducing repeat suicide attempts is only applicable to those at high risk who present to accident and emergency departments. The authors do recognize this, however. The authors focus on repeat suicide attempts as a main outcome. Other outcomes that might be of interest include psychiatric diagnoses, hopelessness, problem-solving ability etc. Additional research is needed in order to ascertain whether the benefits are worth the harms and the costs, however.

Overall, the findings of the review indicated that studies on cognitive-behavioural therapies showed a significant preventative effect on repeated suicidal behaviour. Further research is needed, however, owing to methodological variability in the studies, which may have made results seem too optimistic, before any firm recommendations can be made.

Hawton *et al.* (1998, 2001) identified 23 randomized controlled trials in their review that had investigated psychosocial and/or psychopharmacological treatment versus standard or less intensive types of aftercare, whose primary outcome measured was repetition of deliberate self-harm. The critical appraisal of this study revealed that the review had a clearly focused question, stating that it is a systematic review of randomized controlled trials of psychosocial and physical treatments in preventing repetition of deliberate self-harm. The authors were less clear about the population that they were interested in, however. The search included Medline (1966–1996), PsycLIT (now PsycINFO 1974–1996), Embase (1980–1996) and the Cochrane Controlled Trials Register. Ten journals were also hand searched within the disciplines of psychology and psychiatry and all English journals concerned with suicide. The grey literature was not searched. Inclusion criteria seemed appropriate and the authors attempted to gain additional information on standard aftercare although details are not provided. All studies included were randomized controlled trials. The quality of papers was rated by two independent reviewers, who were blind to authorship. The method of rating used was the quality of concealment of allocation, as recommended by Cochrane. The reviewers attempted to gain missing information from the authors. All reports had been published, but two studies had not been published in full; one was obtained from the author (an unpublished manuscript) and others were published conference proceedings. The overall effect was measured by calculating an odds ratio. No overall effect size is given; studies were divided into the type of treatment.

Generally, results of studies within each group were consistent within themselves. Sensitivity analyses (e.g. omitting trials) did not alter the results. Results therefore seem quite robust. Having divided the studies into the four groups, it seems reasonable to have combined results in each group. Results were clearly displayed and variations in results are discussed and reasons given; the 95% confidence interval was used. The conclusion that there is insufficient evidence to make firm recommendations about the most effective form of treatment does follow from the evidence presented. No sub-group analyses are presented. The studies included patients with a variety of presenting symptoms, so the results should be of relevance to a large number of patients who deliberately harm themselves and need treating in the community. The review only focuses on repetition of deliberate self-harm. Other outcomes that may be of interest include other psychiatric diagnoses such as depression, problem resolution etc. The authors present no cost/risk benefit analysis. They state that more research is needed. Large trials are required in order to confirm the possible benefits of interventions shown in small trials.

Overall, findings indicated that suicide and possible suicide deaths after parasuicide were associated with social class V, unemployment, previous inpatient psychiatric treatment, substance misuse, personality disorder and previous attempted suicide. However, there is still uncertainty about which forms of psychosocial and physical treatments of self-harm patients are most effective. The authors acknowledge certain limitations; for example, that deaths from suicide were only obtained for subjects living in Edinburgh at the time of death. Subjects who had moved away were not taken account of, leading to bias and to acknowledgement that larger trials of treatments associated with trends towards reduced rates of repetition of deliberate self-harm are needed.

Summary points

Most patients who receive treatment for deliberate self-harm will initially have presented to a general hospital, usually for self-poisoning or self-injury. Although a number of treatment options are available, for example, problem-solving therapy, cognitive-behavioural therapy, outreach and intensive therapy and family therapy, the aftercare of deliberate self-harmers can be problematic. This is owing to the low treatment compliance within this group. There have been few intervention studies that have investigated deliberate self-harm in adolescents. These studies also suffer from methodological problems such as using 'all-age' or adult samples. As a result there is little consensus about the most effective type of aftercare for those who engage in deliberate self-harm who do not require residential care.

Two systematic reviews have been carried out looking at the efficacy of psychosocial and pharmacological interventions for deliberate self-harm in adolescence. Hawton *et al.* (1998, 2001) found that there is insufficient evidence to make any firm recommendations about which treatment intervention is most effective in reducing repetition of self-harming behaviour. Promising results have been found in individual studies for problem-solving therapy, dialectical behaviour therapy, depot neuroleptic medication and assertive outreach. Cognitive-behavioural therapies have shown a significant preventative effect on repeated suicidal behaviour. However, further research is needed. In support of this, van der Sande *et al.* (1997) found that studies on cognitive-behavioural therapies showed a significant preventative effect on repeated suicidal behaviour, although the authors again conclude that further research is needed before any firm recommendations can be made.

8 Preventing Adolescent Suicidal Behaviour

Epidemiologically based psychological autopsy studies have provided much of what we know about the characteristics of adolescents who commit suicide. These findings have proved useful in the development of suicide prevention strategies. For example, Diekstra, Kienhorst and Wilds (1995) and Hawton (1996) discuss various approaches to the prevention of suicidal behaviour in young people. These include educational programmes in schools, the control and/or modification of methods used for committing suicide, efforts to reduce substance misuse, responsible media reporting of suicide, specialist services – often crisis intervention – for people seriously contemplating suicide, and aftercare programmes for those who have deliberately harmed themselves. Similarly, Shaffer and Craft (1999) discuss school prevention programmes, method control, media guidelines and crisis hotlines.

School-based educational suicide prevention programmes

Curriculum-based programmes or educational interventions seem to have received most attention in recent years as an approach to suicide prevention. The largest recent growth in educational school-based programmes has been observed in the USA (Garland, Shaffer and Whittle 1989). This has only occurred in a few other countries such as the Netherlands (Mulder, Methorst and Diekstra 1989) and Canada (Dyck 1994). Some school-based education/curricula programmes aim to increase awareness of the problem of suicide and promote the identification of new cases through the description of warning signs and encouragement of disclosure. They also provide information about mental health resources and in some cases improve coping abilities. The programmes are usually presented by a mental health professional or mental health educator. They are mostly aimed at secondary school students, their parents and teachers. A typical programme would include:

1. a review of the epidemiology of adolescent suicide

2. a description of warning signs

3. details of community mental health resources

4. a discussion of how to refer a student or peer to counselling, including confidentiality issues

5. training in communication skills, problem-solving skills and/or stress management.

The theoretical model guiding the curriculum-based prevention programmes is not a mental health model, but a stress model (Garland *et al.* 1989). From this perspective suicide is conceptualized as a reaction of extreme interpersonal or psychosocial stress. The link to mental illness is de-emphasized, in fact it is often explicitly stated that those who commit suicide are not mentally ill. It is also often pointed out that everyone is vulnerable to suicidal behaviour. In this way it is hoped that individuals who are feeling suicidal will be more likely to identify themselves and seek help with the de-stigmatization of suicide.

There are concerns about such programmes, however. They tend to normalize suicidal behaviour, reducing potentially protective taboos. Suicidal behaviour is sometimes portrayed as a reaction to common stresses of adolescence. The incidence of suicidal behaviour is sometimes exaggerated leading to the perception that suicide is more common and therefore more acceptable. It is common to use the media to present case histories so that students can identify friends who might be at risk. However, students may come to identify with the problems portrayed and come to see suicide as a logical solution to their own problems. For example, a rise in the number of suicides was seen in Germany after the broadcast of a documentary on the suicide of an adolescent (Schmidtke and Hafner 1988). Suicide prevention programmes may actually never reach those who are at most risk of suicidal behaviour such as those who do not attend school (Garland and Zigler 1993).

Ploeg *et al.* (1996) have conducted a systematic overview of adolescent suicide prevention programmes. The review was concerned with the efficacy of school-based intervention programmes in preventing suicidal behaviour. Eleven studies were identified that evaluated school-based prevention programmes and had client-focused outcomes and/or cost. The critical appraisal highlighted that the question should be clearly focused, stating that the review aims to summarize evidence of the effectiveness of adolescent suicide prevention curriculum programmes. Bibliographic databases searched were Medline, CINAHL, PsychINFO and the Social Sciences Index 1980–1995. References in 18 relevant journals were also hand searched back to 1980. Inclusion criteria seem clearly defined and appropriate. The validity of relevant articles was assessed using the following criteria:

1. method of allocation

2. level of agreement to participate in the study

3. control for confounding variables

4. method of data collection

5. percentage of subjects available for follow-up.

There was no mention of whether the authors tried to find out missing information from studies. Publication bias is an issue because the grey literature was not searched. There was no explicit measurement of an overall effect size. The authors discuss the results of individual studies relating to suicide risk, knowledge, attitudes, coping, hopelessness and empathy. The results for knowledge about suicide, suicide risk, and hopelessness were fairly consistent from study to study. Attitudes and coping, however, were not consistent from study to study. No explicit detail was given about how results were analyzed. Results were not combined, studies had different outcomes measured. It is difficult to assess the results section due to the lack of methodological detail given and with no confidence intervals presented or discussed. The conclusion that there is insufficient evidence to support curriculum-based prevention programmes for adolescents seems to flow from the evidence presented, however. No sub-group analyses are described. A change in suicidal behaviour might have been a useful outcome to have considered. The authors conclude that more research is needed to demonstrate the impact on the health of adolescents before the question of harms and costs can be tackled.

Overall, there appears to be insufficient evidence to support school-based suicide prevention programmes. In fact, the evidence suggests that the programmes may have both beneficial and harmful effects on some students and that any potential negative effects could have serious consequences. This is particularly true for young males. Programmes increased knowledge about suicide, but positive and negative effects were found on attitudes towards suicide. One study found an increase in hopelessness and maladaptive coping for males as a result of the school-based programme. The increase in knowledge about suicide that has been demonstrated by these programmes, however, seems less important if not accompanied by a change in attitude and suicidal behaviour.

It appears that males are more negatively affected by school-based prevention programmes than females. However, it is not known whether this is due to the content of the programmes themselves or other factors such as the group or school setting benefiting females more than males.

The studies that investigated school-based prevention programmes that were identified by the systematic review conducted by Ploeg et al. (1996) suffered various methodological limitations, which will be important to address for future research. Some studies lacked random assignment of subjects into study groups, others lacked explanation of the method of allocation. Other methodological problems included inadequate control for potential confounders, low subject participation and follow-up rates, testing instruments lacking validity and reliability and short follow-up periods neglecting assessment of long-term effects of the programmes. Clearly, more research is needed in order to establish whether school-based programmes are beneficial.

It seems therefore that not only is there insufficient evidence, but that some of the evidence is conflicting in terms of the effectiveness of school-based suicide prevention programmes. There are also concerns about the focus on suicide in such programmes possibly increasing the attractiveness of suicidal behaviour as an option (Shaffer *et al.* 1990). This has led to programmes focused on mental health issues and coping in general being favoured.

Screening programmes for at-risk individuals in schools

Direct screening for the predictors of suicide in general school populations involves asking students directly and confidentially about whether they are experiencing any depressive symptoms, suicidal ideation or have made a suicide attempt and/or have a substance misuse problem.

There are very few ongoing screening programmes for at-risk individuals in schools. One such programme is the Columbia Teen Screen (Shaffer *et al.* 1996). The programme involves a three-stage screening process. Initially, students complete a brief self-report questionnaire, the Columbia Teen Screen, in a health-related class. Students with an elevated level of risk then go on to complete the DISC, Diagnostic Interview Schedule for Children (Shaffer *et al.* 2000). The third stage involves a face-to-face interview by a clinician in order to determine the need for referral for treatment or further evaluation. The parents of at-risk individuals are then contacted. High risk are those students who report a suicide attempt, suicidal ideation, major depressive disorder or dysthymic disorder or have an alcohol or substance abuse problem. Shaffer *et al.* (1996) examined the efficacy of the Columbia Teen Screen and found that others did not know about the problems of many adolescents who were at high risk and thus had never received treatment. Only 31% with major depressive disorder, 26% with suicidal ideation and 50% who had made a suicide attempt were actually in treatment. Overall, the programme was found to be efficient. As a result, the programme has been conducted for the last ten years and now operates in over 45 sites across the USA (Shaffer and Craft 1999).

Weapon control

The little research that has investigated weapon control indicates that the control of weapons has a negligible effect in decreasing the risk of suicidal behaviour. For example, Cummings *et al.* (1997) investigated the impact of gun-safe storage laws on gun-related deaths in children under 15 years of age. They found no decrease in gun-related suicide rates.

Crisis intervention centres

Crisis intervention centres generally provide a 24-hour hotline and referral to other mental health or social work agency services. The rationale for such centres is that suicidal behaviour is often associated with a crisis situation where an individual is ambivalent about living or dying. People have a basic need for interpersonal communication, which is often expressed as a last minute 'cry for help'. The growth of these crisis intervention services really began in the early 1960s with the establishment of the Samaritans in London and the first suicide prevention centre in Los Angeles. They have the potential to have a positive effect on mental state at a time of stress. However, research indicates that they have little effect in reducing suicide rates within the community (Apsler and Hodas 1976; Bleach and Clairborn 1974; Miller *et al.* 1984; Shaffer *et al.* 1990).

Evaluation of the centres has also looked at whether they attract individuals who are at high risk for suicidal behaviour and whether they prevent these persons from attempting or committing suicide (Bridge *et al.* 1977; Dew *et al.* 1987; Lester 1972). Dew *et al.* (1987) carried out a meta-analysis and found that these centres do attract high-risk populations. However, it remains unclear whether suicide prevention centres actually decrease the rate of suicide in the communities where they are based.

Reduction of substance abuse

Research has indicated a strong association between substance abuse and suicidal behaviour. Prevention of alcohol and drug abuse in young people, for example through educational measures, should lead to a reduction in suicidal behaviour. It is important that the assessment of young suicide attempters should include careful screening for substance abuse. Close links between substance abuse and general hospital services also need to be developed so that specialist treatment is available for those who attempt suicide and abuse drugs or alcohol.

More responsible media reporting

There has been some evidence put forward that suicides in young people may be facilitated by dramatic reports or dramas by the media. In fact Diekstra and Garnefski (1995) have suggested that the increase in suicidal behaviour among adolescents is due to the more frequent presentation of positive suicide models by the media. The media should therefore be made aware of this and their presentation of these events be more responsible, for example not mentioning the actual methods used when reporting in newspapers or the television. It is also important for programmes including material about suicidal behaviour to be followed by helpline information, and expert advice should be sought when planning programmes of this nature.

The World Health Organisation (1993) put forward a number of points to aid the prevention of suicidal behaviour with respect to media reporting. It was stated that it was important to avoid sensational reporting, stories should not be reported on the front pages of newspapers, no photographs should be included, suicidal behaviour should not be described as an understandable way of problem-solving and the addresses and phone numbers of helping agencies such as hotlines and the Samaritans should also be presented with the article. These proposals are now widely accepted and have been adopted by a number of suicide prevention organizations such as the International Association for Suicide Prevention, the American Association for Suicidology, including the associations for suicide prevention in Germany, Austria and Switzerland.

Prevention of repetition of self-harm

Deliberate self-harm often becomes an habitual way of coping with stress. This particularly applies to self-cutting. A number of strategies may help prevent it. These include understanding, minimization, distraction, avoidance, deterrence and talking. It is important to understand why and when a person self-harms. Minimization reduces the seriousness of the act of deliberate self-harm, for example, making a small cut rather than a big one. Some individuals will find it effective to distract themselves from the act of self-harming by doing something else. Others will find avoidance an effective technique, for example, not keeping razor blades or other sharp objects in the house. In contrast, for some keeping the item used to self-harm in constant view as a reminder not to use may be effective and often talking to someone who is seen as 'safe' may help.

Summary points

A number of approaches for the prevention of suicidal behaviour in adolescents can be found. For example, educational programmes in schools, screening programmes for at-risk individuals in schools, the control of methods used for committing suicide, efforts to reduce substance misuse, media guidelines and crisis hotlines. The effectiveness of some of these methods of suicide prevention remains questionable, however. Educational programmes in schools have been found to have both beneficial and harmful effects on suicidal behaviour in adolescents. Clearly, more research is needed to clarify this issue. There is evidence that discreet screening for the predictors of suicidal behaviour in general may be a better approach to adopt.

9 Future Prospects

This book is a collation of information on deliberate self-harm in adolescence. More specifically, it provides data on the prevalence of suicidal behaviour in adolescents, discusses risk factors, screening instruments, outcome, management and the prevention of suicidal behaviour. This information is backed up by the critical appraisal of research papers related to the efficacy of aftercare and its outcome, screening instruments for the identification of at-risk individuals, links of suicidal behaviour with various psychiatric disorders and child to adult follow-up.

Conclusions

It has become clear that there are a number of important issues within the field of adolescent suicidal behaviour. A large number of different terms have arisen within the literature to describe suicidal behaviour, for example deliberate self-harm, self-injurious behaviour, attempted suicide, parasuicide, self-cutting, self-poisoning etc. This has led to confusion. Suicidal behaviour has also been described in terms of suicidal intent, increasing the debate. The variation in the way that terms are defined has in part caused problems for epidemiological research. Inconsistencies in the way that data are collected and coded, the subjective nature of identifying a death as suicide and the fact that not all cases come into contact with the emergency services has also meant that data relating to the prevalence of deliberate self-harm are problematic. In fact, available data are thought to underestimate the size of the problem. The development of standardized criteria for identifying deliberate self-harm and its different types of acts would enable improved data for epidemiological and other research. The DSM and ICD systems could productively be used, as at the present time neither provides diagnostic criteria for the identification of deliberate self-harm.

A number of biological, psychological and sociological factors have been identified that are thought to increase the risk of suicidal behaviour. For example, deficits in problem-solving, impulsivity, feelings of hopelessness, anger and hostility, having a psychiatric disorder, family characteristics such as lone parent families and disturbed family relationships and the media. It is assumed that the cause of suicidal behaviour is multifactorial and lies with an association between risk factors. Much attention has been given to the investigation of links between suicidal behaviour and psychiatric diagnoses. As a result, suicidal behaviour in adolescence has been linked to depression, substance abuse and conduct disorder. Substantial evidence has also arisen to support the notion that the reporting of suicidal behaviour in newspapers plays a contributory part to suicidal behaviour in young people.

Research into the causality of suicidal behaviour has been consistent in its results, however much of the research is problematic. That is, it has suffered from small sample sizes, a lack of generalizability of results and limitations owing to methods of data collection. Suicidal acts are relatively rare, even in high-risk groups; small sample sizes are therefore particularly problematic within this field (Hawton and van Heeringen 2000). It is important to employ large-scale, longitudinal investigation since it is a more informative and powerful approach. It is also important to establish more knowledge about the relative contribution made by the differing risk factors. For example, whether there is a chronological pattern of development of comorbidity of disorders, which would in turn aid in treatment (Hawton and van Heeringen 2000). The reporting of suicidal behaviour by the media should make clear the association between suicidal behaviour and mental health problems and should be accompanied by information on how to access sources of help. The psychological autopsy method has provided a wealth of knowledge about the risk factors of suicide. However, the extent and quality of information that can be obtained through using this approach is limited. That is, the range of factors that can be examined are limited. For example, the approach does not allow the investigation of the underlying psychological mechanisms that lead to suicide or a suicide attempt, and the extent to which biological factors can be investigated is restricted. The investigation of survivors of serious suicide attempts would overcome these problems, where the suicidal thinking process could be examined through the follow-up of patients. In this way biological, psychological and social factors could be investigated. This does raise the issue of the definition of what a 'serious' suicide attempt would entail, where strict criteria would need to be developed and adhered to.

Within the last ten years there has been a large growth in interest in the assessment of young people thought to be at risk of suicidal behaviour. As a result, numerous screening instruments for the identification of at-risk adolescents have been developed. Recently, however, more attention has been given to developing new instruments rather than evaluating the utility of existing tools (Goldston 2000). In particular, it is important to investigate the predictive validity of existing assessment instruments using a prospective design and to examine discriminate validity of the tools (the degree to which suicidal behaviour does not correlate with constructs that it should not). Screening instruments for identifying at-risk adolescents should not, however, be used as the sole or primary means of risk assessment, but in clinical work with adolescents have a useful adjunctive role.

The majority of patients who receive treatment for deliberate self-harm will usually initially have presented to a general hospital, most commonly for self-poisoning or self-injury. A number of treatment options are available for patients who deliberately self-harm. For example, problem-solving therapy, cognitive-behavioural therapy, outreach and intensive therapy and family therapy. The aftercare of deliberate self-harmers can be problematic owing to the low treatment compliance within this group. There have been few intervention studies that have investigated deliberate self-harm in adolescents. Promising results have been found in individual studies for problem-solving therapy, dialectical behaviour therapy, depot neuroleptic medication and assertive outreach. Cognitive-behavioural therapies have also been shown to have a significant preventative effect on repeated suicidal behaviour (Hawton *et al.* 1998, 2001; van der Sande *et al.* 1997). However, further research is needed in order to make any firm recommendations as the research that has been conducted suffers from methodological problems. Studies have small sample sizes, have utilized 'all-age' or adult samples limiting generalizability of results to adolescent populations and included poor descriptions of the content of treatment, especially in the control condition. As a result there is little consensus about the type of aftercare needed for those who engage in deliberate self-harm. Larger sample sizes are needed, which may involve data collection across multiple centres or even multiple countries. This would also aid with the generalizability of results obtained.

Young people who engage in self-harming behaviour come into contact with a large number of differing professionals, and as such require a range of agencies and sectors of care. These include doctors and nurses in accident and emergency departments, psychiatrists, paediatricians and psychologists. Interdisciplinary liaison and co-operation is essential for good clinical practice when delivering services. General hospital and aftercare services should be delivered according to recommended standards. In commissioning services for adolescents who deliberately self-harm, it is important to identify the relevant resources based on local assessments of need, taking into account the national position. Immediate and long-term physical and mental health care with respect to assessment, admission and continuing care all need to be catered for.

The future outlook for adolescents who engage in non-fatal self-harming behaviour is unclear. Following an act of deliberate self-harm, there is some suggestion that there is an increased risk of suicide and an increased risk of repetition of deliberate self-harm. A small body of research cites an increased risk of later personality disturbance such as repeated separations, poor social problem-solving and impaired peer relationships. However, very little research has been conducted which specifically follows up children and adolescents who exhibit suicidal behaviour into adulthood, limiting conclusions that can be made.

Approaches for the prevention of suicidal behaviour in adolescents have included educational programmes in schools, screening programmes for at-risk individuals in schools, the control of methods used for committing suicide, efforts to reduce substance misuse, media guidelines and crisis hotlines. The effectiveness of some of these methods of suicide prevention remains questionable, however. For example, educational programmes in schools have been found to have both beneficial and harmful effects on suicidal behaviour in adolescents. Research will need to clarify which components of the programmes are favourable and which are detrimental. There is some evidence that discreet screening for the predictors of suicidal behaviour in general may be a better approach to adopt. This raises an important issue in the prevention of suicidal behaviour: whether to target the general population or high-risk groups. Hawton and van Heeringen (2000) propose a combination approach. Prevention strategies should be partly directed at the factors that increase the risk of suicide in the general population, for example media portrayal of suicidal behaviour and availability of methods, and partly at high-risk groups, for example suicide attempters or patients with certain comorbid mental health problems such as depression.

Messages to take away

There are a number of key messages that have become apparent within the field of adolescent suicidal behaviour as a result of writing this book:

- At the present time there is no consensus about the use of a common term and the confusion of terminology remains.

- There are no diagnostic criteria for deliberate self-harm or suicidal behaviour.

- The prevalence figures that are available are thought to greatly underestimate the numbers of adolescents who engage in deliberate self-harm each year.

- Suicidal behaviour has been linked to depression, substance abuse and conduct disorder, however there is a lack of robust research to substantiate such claims.

- There are a number of screening instruments for the identification of at-risk adolescents. In clinical work with adolescents they can have a useful adjunctive role but should not be used as the sole or primary means of assessing risk.

- There is some suggestion that there is an increased risk of suicide and an increased risk of repetition of deliberate self-harm following an act of deliberate self-harm. However, little research has specifically followed up children and adolescents who exhibit suicidal behaviour into adulthood meaning that the long-term outcome for children and adolescents who engage in non-fatal deliberate self-harm is unclear.

- There is little consensus as to the type of aftercare needed for adolescents who deliberately self-harm, owing to insufficient evidence on which to base any firm recommendations about the effectiveness of different treatment interventions.

- There are a number of approaches to the prevention of suicidal behaviour in young people. Research has provided insufficient evidence to support school-based educational suicide prevention programmes. Discreet systematic screening of the predictors of suicide in general school populations, or a combination approach targeting general and high-risk populations may be more desirable.

Future research

Although there has been a growing volume of research on adolescent suicide and deliberate self-harm within the last decade, more research is needed. Future research needs to:

- further evaluate the utility of existing screening instruments for the identification of at-risk children and adolescents

- investigate the impact of management of attempted suicide patients during the initial stages of treatment by staff in accident and emergency departments

- develop a greater understanding of the reasons why many choose to leave hospital before management has been completed, in order to increase treatment compliance

- investigate which psychotherapeutic interventions are most effective

- clarify which school-based educational prevention programmes are beneficial

- investigate the links between suicidal behaviour and depression, substance abuse and antisocial behaviour
- follow up those who exhibit suicidal behaviour in adolescence in order to answer questions about the outcome of deliberate self-harm.

Overall, research needs to increase sample sizes and specifically concentrate on the adolescent population. Findings of research incorporating adult subjects may not be readily generalizable to young people.

Resources

The Camelot Foundation
11-13 Lower Grosvenor Place
London SW1W 0EX
020 7828 6085
www.camelotfoundation.org.uk

Centre for Evidence-Based Mental Health
Department of Psychiatry
University of Oxford
Warneford Hospital
Oxford OX3 7JX
01865 266 476
www.cebmh.com

Centre for Reviews and Dissemination
University of York
York YO10 5DD
01904 321 040
www.york.ac.uk/inst/crd

Mental Health Foundation
83 Victoria Street
London SW1H 0HW
020 7802 0300
www.mentalhealth.org.uk

MIND (National Association for Mental Health)
Granta House
15–19 Broadway
London E15 4BQ
0208 519 2122
www.mind.org.uk

National Children's Bureau
8 Wakley Street
London EC1V 7QE
020 7843 6000
www.ncb.org.uk

National Self-Harm Network
PO Box 7264
Nottingham NG1 6WJ
www.selfharm.org.uk

YoungMinds
102–108 Clerkenwell Road
London EC1M 5SA
020 7336 8445
www.youngminds.org.uk

Young People and Self Harm: A National Inquiry
The Mental Health Foundation and the Camelot Foundation are conducting an investigation into self harm and young people.
www.selfharmUK.org

The Young People and Self-Harm Information Resource website
www.ncb.org.uk/projects/selfharm.htm

Appendix

Evidence-based practice is defined as the 'conscientious, explicit and judicious use of the current best evidence in making decisions about the care of individual patients' (Sackett *et al.* 1996). It involves finding and examining new evidence and integrating it into services and the care of individual patients (Ramchandani, Joughin and Zwi 2001). FOCUS is a child and adolescent mental health project that aims to promote evidence-based practice in child and adolescent mental health services (CAMHS). It accomplishes this through the dissemination of information. FOCUS produces evidence-based publications, which review the existing literature and critically appraise research in order to establish the quality of the research base with respect to different topic areas within CAMHS. This book was written with this aim in mind. In order to produce an evidence-based publication such as this one, or to conduct evidence-based research in a subject area relevant to your own professional practice, there are four stages:

1. The literature needs to be searched.

2. Criteria should be drawn up to include only papers that are relevant to the particular topic area.

3. The type of research then needs to be established.

4. Criteria should be drawn up for which papers are to be critically appraised in order to ascertain the quality of the research.

Searching the literature

The best databases to search initially are Medline, which indexes over 4000 journals covering nursing, psychiatry, psychology, biochemistry and health care management and PsychINFO, which covers the fields of psychology, medicine, psychiatry, nursing, sociology, education, pharmacology, physiology and linguistics. A number of different companies supply these databases, with Ovid Technologies (OVID) and Silver Platter Information (WinSPIRS) being two of the most common. It is also important to search the Cochrane Library, which is a collection of databases published on-line. It consists of the Cochrane Database of Systematic Reviews (CDSR), the DARE (a collection of abstracts of quality-assessed references), the Cochrane Controlled Trials Register (CCTR) and the Cochrane Review Methodology Database.

In order to carry out a focused and appropriate search, it is important to first define a population or type of patient or client (age, gender, diagnosis etc.), an intervention or exposure and an outcome of interest. For example: 'Do psychosocial interventions (intervention) reduce repetition (outcome) of deliberate self-harm in adolescents (population)?'

There are two ways in which you can search for articles having defined your search question: by text word or by what are called 'MeSH' headings.

If you search by *text word*, it is important to remember that the database will be searched for the exact term entered. All possible spellings and terms associated with, or describing each of the components of the search question (topic, population, intervention and outcome) need to be considered. For example, deliberate self-harm can also be termed 'attempted suicide', 'self-harm', 'parasuicide', 'self-injurious behaviour' etc. Adolescents can also be described as 'young people', 'teenagers' etc.

The results of the search will give you references stored on the database within which the word or term searched for can be found. When typing in a search term, *Boolean operators* can play an important role. Boolean operators combine keywords in a search strategy. For example, 'and' links together different subjects, focusing the search and allowing the retrieval of fewer papers. The search term 'deliberate self-harm *and* adolescents' will only identify papers that address both deliberate self-harm and the adolescent population. Entering 'or' will allow you to broaden your search. The search 'deliberate self-harm *or* attempted suicide' will identify papers that address either deliberate self-harm or attempted suicide or both. The word 'not' is another Boolean operator, but should be used with care. 'Adolescents *not* adults' would exclude papers about adults. *Truncation* is another important tool. Truncation means that by typing the word 'random*', the database search would identify papers with the terms 'randomised', 'randomized', 'randomisation' and 'randomization' in them. It is important to note that the characters that are used are different for Silver Platter and OVID versions, with Silver Platter using '*' and OVID using '$'.

Medline and PsychINFO also make use of a thesaurus to make searching more effective. The thesaurus indexes information from journals by grouping related words and concepts using a single preferred term. The thesaurus used by Medline and the Cochrane Library is called MeSH. This thesaurus contains 17,000 terms, which each represent a single concept that appears in the literature. For Silver Platter, MeSH headings can be identified by checking the thesaurus or using the 'suggest' option. For OVID, a 'mapping' procedure will enable the identification of the MeSH terms. If a MeSH term that matches your subject cannot be found then the search will need to be carried out using text words.

It is also possible to search for articles using pre-existing search strategies. These enable the identification of particular types of study within a topic area. For example, for this book, existing search strategies were used in order to identify systematic reviews, meta-analyses and randomized controlled trials (see section headed Quality of research for an explanation of these different study designs). A number of search strategies have been developed by the Cochrane Collaboration that enable the searcher to simply type in the search framework developed, adding in search terms relevant to their search topic where required. It is important to note that a number of different companies supply the various databases, so different commands are required depending on the supplier. Ovid Technologies (OVID) and Silver Platter Information (WinSPIRS) are two of the most common suppliers for which search strategies have been developed. These can be found in Boxes A.1 to A.5.

Box A.1 Silver Platter systematic review and meta-analysis search strategy

1. (subject search strategy)
2. (TG=ANIMAL) not ((TG=HUMAN) and (TG=ANIMAL))
3. #1 not #2
4. REVIEW-ACADEMIC in PT
5. REVIEW-TUTORIAL in PT
6. META-ANALYSIS in PT
7. META-ANALYSIS
8. SYSTEMATIC* near REVIEW*
9. SYSTEMATIC* near OVERVIEW*
10. META-ANALY* or METAANALY* or (META ANALY*)
11. #10 in TI
12. #10 in AB
13. #4 or #5 or #6 or #7 or #8 or #9 or #11 or #12
14. #3 and #13

For actual search example see Table A.2.

Box A.2 OVID systematic review and meta-analysis search strategy (high sensitivity, low precision)

1.	meta.ab.	17.	reviewed.ab.
2.	synthesis.ab.	18.	english.ab.
3.	literature.ab.	19.	language.ab.
4.	randomized.hw.	20.	comment.pt.
5.	published.ab.	21.	letter.pt.
6.	meta-analysis.pt.	22.	editorial.pt.
7.	extraction.ab.	23.	animal/
8.	trials.hw.	24.	human/
9.	controlled.hw.	25.	#23 not (#23 and #24)
10.	medline.ab.	26.	(YOUR SUBJECT TERMS)
11.	selection.ab.	27.	#26 not (#20 or #21 or #22 or #25)
12.	sources.ab.		
13.	trials.ab.	28.	or/#1–19
14.	review.ab.	29.	#27 and #28
15.	review.pt.		
16.	articles.ab.		

Box A.3 OVID systematic review and meta-analysis search strategy (low sensitivity, high precision)

1.	medline.ab.	7.	#5 not (#5 and #6)
2.	comment.pt.	8.	(YOUR SUBJECT TERMS)
3.	letter.pt.	9.	#8 not (#2 or #3 or #4 or #7)
4.	editorial.pt.		
5.	animal/	10.	#1 and #9
6.	human/		

Box A.4 OVID randomized controlled trial search strategy

1. RANDOMIZED CONTROLLED TRIAL.pt.
2. CONTROLLED CLINICAL TRIAL.pt.
3. RANDOMIZED CONTROLLED TRIALS.sh.
4. RANDOM ALLOCATION.sh.
5. DOUBLE BLIND METHOD.sh.
6. SINGLE-BLIND METHOD.sh.
7. or/#1–6
8. ANIMAL.sh. not HUMAN.sh.
9. #7 not #8
10. CLINICAL TRIAL.pt.
11. exp CLINICAL TRIALS
12. (clin$ adj25 trial$).ti,ab.
13. ((singl$ or doubl$ or trebl$ or tripl$) adj25 (blind$ or mask$)).ti,ab.
14. PLACEBOS.sh.
15. placebo$.ti,ab.
16. random$.ti,ab.
17. RESEARCH DESIGN.sh.
18. or/#10–17
19. #18 not #8
20. #19 not #9
21. COMPARATIVE STUDY.sh.
22. exp EVALUATION STUDIES
23. FOLLOW UP STUDIES.sh.
24. PROSPECTIVE STUDIES.sh.
25. (control$ or prospectiv$ or volunteer$).ti,ab.
26. or/#21–25
27. #26 not #8
28. #26 not (#9 or #20)
29. #9 or #20 or #28

Box A.5 Silver Platter randomized controlled trial search strategy

1. (Subject search strategy)

2. (TG= ANIMAL) not ((TG=HUMAN) and (TG=ANIMAL))

3. #1 not #2

4. RANDOMIZED-CONTROLLED-TRIAL in PT

5. CONTROLLED-CLINICAL-TRIAL in PT

6. RANDOMIZED-CONTROLLED-TRIALS

7. RANDOM-ALLOCATION

8. DOUBLE-BLIND-METHOD

9. SINGLE-BLIND-METHOD

10. CLINICAL-TRIAL in PT

11. explode CLINICAL-TRIALS/ALL SUBHEADINGS

12. (clin* near trial*) in TI

13. (clin* near trial*) in AB

14. (singl* or doubl* or trebl* or tripl*) near (blind* or mask*)

15. (#14 in TI) or (#14 in AB)

16. PLACEBOS

17. placebo* in TI

18. placebo* in AB

19. random* in TI

20. random* in AB

21. RESEARCH-DESIGN

22. TG=COMPARATIVE-STUDY

23. explode EVALUATION-STUDIES/ALL SUBHEADINGS

24. FOLLOW-UP-STUDIES

25. PROSPECTIVE-STUDIES

26. control* or prospectiv* or volunteer*

27. (#26 in TI) or (#26 in AB)

28. #4 or #5 or #6 or #7 or #8 or #9

29. #10 or #11 or #12 or #13 or #15 or #16 or #17 or #18 or #19 or #20 or #21

30. #22 or #23 or #24 or #25 or #27

31. #28 or #29 or #30

32. #3 and #31

The existing search strategies that were used for this book were those developed by the Cochrane Collaboration for Medline and PsychINFO using Silver Platter technology in order to identify systematic reviews, meta-analyses and randomized controlled trials. Table A.1 shows the search strategy results for the Medline search for systematic reviews and meta-analyses (Silver Platter) and Table A.2 the search strategy results for the Medline search for randomized controlled trials (Silver Platter). The search results themselves show the request or line number, the number of records identified and the search request made. As a result, figures are interpreted as follows. In Table A.1, line number four, 285 records were found when the search request of 'self-harm' was typed in to the Medline database search. This search provided a total of 127 studies that matched the filtered search criteria.

Table A.1 Medline search for systematic reviews and meta-analyses (Silver Platter)

No.	Records	Request
1	137	deliberate self harm
2	3049	'Suicide,-Attempted'/all subheadings
3	102	deliberate self-harm
4	285	self harm
5	223	self-harm
6	156	parasuicide
7	114	self destructive behav*
8	310	self-injurious behav*
9	937	suicid* behav*
10	310	self injury
11	4292	#1 or #2 or #3 or #4 or #5 or #6 or #7 or #8 or #9 or #10
12	304658	adoles*
13	2220	young people
14	441	young person*
15	3956	teen*
16	305990	#12 or #13 or #14 or #15
17	1696	#11 and #16
18	814751	(TG=animal) not ((tg=human) and (tg =animal))
19	1696	#17 not #18
20	41537	review-academic in pt
21	371190	review-tutorial in pt
22	4704	meta-analysis in pt
23	6034	meta-analysis
24	2217	systematic* near review*
25	159	systematic* near overview*
26	6910	meta-analy* or metaanaly* or (meta analy*)
27	2924	#26 in ti
28	4641	#26 in ab
29	420433	#20 or #21 or #22 or #23 or #24 or #25 or #27 or #28
*30	127	#19 and #29

(For template see Box A.1.)

Table A.2 Medline search for randomized controlled trials (Silver Platter)

No.	Records	Request
1	76	deliberate self harm
2	1202	'Suicide,-Attempted'/all subheadings
3	54	deliberate self-harm
4	153	self harm
5	121	self-harm
6	49	parasuicide
7	41	self destructive behav*
8	146	self-injurious behav*
9	403	suicid* behav*
10	128	self injury
11	1753	#1 or #2 or #3 or #4 or #5 or #6 or #7 or #8 or #9 or #10
12	119575	adoles*
13	1027	young people
14	183	young person*
15	1716	teen*
16	120146	#12 or #13 or #14 or #15
17	679	#11 and #16
18	300506	(TG=animal) not ((tg=human) and (tg =animal))
19	679	#17 not #18
20	36738	RANDOMIZED-CONTROLLED-TRIAL in PT
21	8543	CONTROLLED-CLINICAL-TRIAL in PT
22	0	RANDOMIZED-CONTROLLED-TRIALS
23	5373	RANDOM-ALLOCATION
24	13829	DOUBLE-BLIND-METHOD
25	2299	SINGLE-BLIND-METHOD
26	76443	CLINICAL-TRIAL in PT
27	19059	explode CLINICAL-TRIALS/ALL SUBHEADINGS
28	3430	(clin* near trial*) in TI
29	16120	(clin* near trial*) in AB
30	18139	(singl* or doubl* or trebl* or tripl*) near (blind* or mask*)

Continued on next page

Table A.2 continued

No.	Records	Request
31	12686	(#30 in TI) or (#30 in AB)
32	2383	PLACEBOS
33	2256	placebo* in TI
34	15068	placebo* in AB
35	8701	random* in TI
36	58885	random* in AB
37	4722	RESEARCH-DESIGN
38	148435	TG=COMPARATIVE-STUDY
39	67388	explode EVALUATION-STUDIES/ALL SUBHEADINGS
40	49952	FOLLOW-UP-STUDIES
41	39111	PROSPECTIVE-STUDIES
42	347183	control* or prospectiv* or volunteer*
43	258696	(#42 in TI) or (#42 in AB)
44	52457	#20 or #21 or #22 or #23 or #24 or #25
45	135291	#26 or #27 or #28 or #29 or #31 or #32 or #33 or #34 or #35 or #36 or #37
46	447124	#38 or #39 or #40 or #41 or #43
47	494054	#44 or #45 or #46
*48	287	#19 and #47

(For template see Box A.5.)

Once the search results have been obtained, the reduced number of studies produced can be individually assessed for relevance and further filtered. It is also important that in addition to searching Medline and PsychINFO, the reference lists of papers that were identified through the literature search are checked for any journal articles that may have been missed. Having carried out the literature search, when producing an evidence-based piece of work, the quality of the papers identified needs then to be assessed.

Quality of research

Research evidence is conceptualized in a hierarchy. A high-quality systematic review or meta-analysis constitutes the best available evidence, found at the top of the hierarchy. Case studies and individual opinion form the least robust form of evidence on the other hand and are found at the bottom of the hierarchy. The hierarchy of evidence is illustrated in Box A.6.

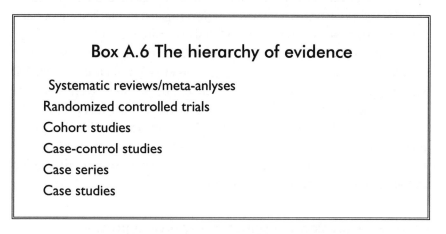

Box A.6 The hierarchy of evidence

Systematic reviews/meta-anlyses
Randomized controlled trials
Cohort studies
Case-control studies
Case series
Case studies

A systematic review locates and appraises evidence using systematic criteria in order to minimize error and bias. *Meta-analyses* merge and re-analyze study results, where studies are sufficiently similar and robust. In this way, it is possible to achieve a reliable overview of the research in question. A *randomized controlled trial* involves subjects being randomly allocated to either a treatment or control group. Information relating to the effectiveness of the intervention is obtained through the comparison of the two groups. *Cohort studies* usually take the form of prospective epidemiological studies. They usually involve two groups of individuals who vary in their exposure to an intervention or hazard. The groups are then followed to assess outcome and estimate the association between exposure and outcome. These studies can also be conducted retrospectively. *Case-control studies* are usually retrospective in nature. They are used to investigate the causes of disease. They involve the comparison of subjects who have been affected by disease with those who have not. A record is made of the differences in the presence or absence of hypothesized risk factors. *Case series* are uncontrolled, observational studies that involve an intervention and an outcome for more than one person. *Case studies* are also uncontrolled observational studies, however they involve an intervention and outcome for only one person (NHS Centre for Reviews and

Dissemination, CRD Report 4 1996; Cochrane Collaboration Handbook 1996).

Criteria for considering papers

Once papers have been identified, although reduced in number, they will need then to be further screened for relevance. For example, the studies identified for this book were retained if they investigated the adolescent population; the target age range was early adolescence through to 19 years of age, but studies that involved young people up to the age of 24 were also included. Only empirical studies that either used a control group or included within-group comparisons between levels of suicidal symptoms, for example suicide attempters versus suicide ideators, were retained. Studies were limited to those written in the English language that had been conducted within the last ten years. Inclusion and/or exclusion criteria are normally devised by the researcher and can be broad or specific, depending on the requirements of the piece of work.

Criteria for considering papers for critical appraisal

In order to ascertain the quality of the research identified, papers can be critically appraised. A range of critical appraisal tools have been developed because different questions need to be addressed depending on the type of methodology used. Tables A.3–A.7 show the different types of critical appraisal tools that are available.

Table A.3 Critical appraisal tool
for systematic reviews and meta-analyses

Systematic reviews/meta-analyses
Author/s:
Title of paper:
Date:
Design:
Outcomes measured:
Principal outcomes:
Are the results valid?
Is the question clearly focused?
Is the search thorough?
Is the validity of included studies adequately assessed?
What are the results?
How big is the overall effect?
Are the results consistent from study to study?
If the results of the review have been combined, was it reasonable to do so?
How precise are the results?
Interpretation of the results – will they help in making decisions about patients?
Do conclusions flow from evidence that is reviewed?
Are sub-groups' analyses interpreted cautiously?
Can the conclusions and data be generalized to other settings?
Were all important outcomes considered?
Are the benefits worth the harms and the costs?
Comments:

(Adapted from material produced by the Centre for Evidence-Based Mental Health. See Resources)

Table A.4 Critical appraisal tool for randomized controlled trials

Randomized controlled trials
Author/s:
Title of paper:
Date:

Are the results of this trial valid?
Are you using the right research paper to answer your particular question?
Was the group of patients clearly defined? Consider: the population studied comorbidity classification used outcomes measured.
Was the assignment of patients to treatments randomized? Was the randomization list concealed?
Were all patients who entered the trial accounted for at its conclusion?
Were they analyzed in the groups to which they were randomized?
Were patients and clinicians kept 'blind' to which treatment was being received?
Aside from the experimental treatment, were the groups treated equally?
If a cross-over design is used are attempts made to reduce the carry-over effects? Did the authors acknowledge that this was a potential problem? Was an appropriate washout period used?

Continued on next page

Table A.4 continued

What are the results?	
How large was the treatment effect? (See 'Guidance for calculating numbers needed to treat'.)	
How precise is the estimate of treatment effect? (See 'Guidance for calculating intervals'.)	
What are the implications of this paper for local practice?	
Are the results of this study generalizable to your patient? Does your patient resemble those in the study? What are your patient's preferences? Are there alternative treatments available?	

(Adapted from material produced by the Centre for Evidence-Based Mental Health. See Resources)

Guidance for calculating Numbers Needed to Treat (NNT)

Numbers Needed to Treat (NNT) represents the number of patients you need to treat in order to prevent one negative outcome.

1. ESTABLISH THE CONTROL EVENT RATE (CER)

The Control Event Rate (CER) is the proportion of patients in the study's control group experiencing the observed negative event.

Enter the CER for your study in the box:

CER =

2. ESTABLISH THE EXPERIMENTAL EVENT RATE (EER)

The Experimental Event Rate (EER) is the proportion of patients in the study's experimental group (i.e. the group receiving the experimental treatment) experiencing the observed negative event.

Enter the EER for your study in the box:

EER =

3. CALCULATE THE ABSOLUTE RISK REDUCTION (ARR)

The Absolute Risk Reduction (ARR) is the absolute difference in the risk of an adverse outcome between the control group and the experimental group. It is calculated by deducting the EER from the CER. Perform this calculation now:

> ARR =   (CER from above) –   (EER from above) =

4) CALCULATE THE NUMBER NEEDED TO TREAT (NNT)

The Number Needed to Treat (NNT), defined above, is calculated by dividing the ARR into 1 and multiplying the result by 100.

Perform this calculation now:

> NNT = 1 ÷   (ARR from above) x 100 =

Worked example

A population of 200 patients was divided into an experimental and a control group with 100 patients in each. The experimental group was given haloperidol in order to prevent recurrence of psychotic episodes. Ten patients in the experimental group experienced a psychotic episode during the period of the trial. Thirty five patients in the control group experienced a psychotic episode during the period of the trial.

1. ESTABLISH THE CONTROL EVENT RATE (CER)

Thirty five patients experienced the event out of a population of 100, therefore the CER will be 35%.

> CER = 35%

2. ESTABLISH THE EXPERIMENTAL EVENT RATE (EER)

Ten patients experienced the event out of a population of 100, therefore the EER will be 10%.

> EER = 10%

3. CALCULATE THE ABSOLUTE RISK REDUCTION (ARR)

In this example, the CER equals 35% and the EER equals 10%.

ARR = 35 (CER from above) − 10 (EER from above) = 25%

4. CALCULATE THE NUMBER NEEDED TO TREAT (NNT)

In our sample data, the ARR equals 25%.

NNT = 1 ÷ 25 (ARR from above) × 100 = 4

Guidance for calculating Confidence Intervals (CIs)

The Confidence Interval (CI) gives the range within which we would expect the true value of a statistical measure to lie. Most research studies use a CI of 95% e.g. an NNT of 10 with a 95% CI of 5 to 15 would give us 95% confidence that the true NNT value was between 5 and 15.

The formula for calculating a 95% Confidence Interval on an NNT is:

$$+/-1.96 \sqrt{\frac{\text{CER x } (1 - \text{CER})}{\text{\# of control patients}} + \frac{\text{EER x } (1 - \text{EER})}{\text{\# of exper. pts.}}}$$

Please note: in the formula the CER and EER are expressed as fractions, rather than percentages. For example, a 25% CER is expressed as 0.25.

Enter the figures for your study into the formula:

$$+/-1.96 \sqrt{\frac{...... \text{ x } (1 - ....)}{............} + \frac{...... \text{ x } (1 - ....)}{............}}$$

This will give you the percentage range within which the truly accurate NNT can be found. The smaller the percentage, the more confident you can be that the NNT is accurate.

Table A.5 Critical appraisal tool for cohort studies

Cohort studies	
Author/s:	
Title of paper:	
Date:	
Outcomes measured:	
Principal outcomes:	
Are the exposed people representative of the standard users of the intervention?	
Was the non-exposed cohort selected from the same population as the exposed?	
Was exposure reliably ascertained and verified?	
What factors (other than the exposure) may affect the outcome?	
Were the cohorts comparable on these important confounding factors?	
Was there adequate adjustment for the effects of these confounding variables?	
Was a dose-response relationship between exposure and outcome demonstrated?	
Was outcome assessment blind to exposure status?	
Was follow-up long enough for the outcomes to occur?	
Was an adequate proportion of the cohort followed up?	
Were drop-out rates similar in exposed and unexposed groups?	
Comments:	

(Adapted from material produced by the NHS Centre for Reviews and Dissemination. See Resources)

Table A.6 Critical appraisal tool for case-control studies

Case control studies	
Author:	
Study:	
Date:	
Design:	
Outcomes measured:	
Principal outcomes:	
Is the information from the past dependable? Are data available from well-documented medical records with data recorded in a reliable method?	
If data has been recorded based on the recollection of subjects, is recall bias operating? What attempts have the authors made to assess the effect of this potential bias?	
How alike are the control group? Are they really from a similar population differing only in the absence of disease?	
Are there any other differences that might have a bearing on the outcome being studied? Have matching techniques been used in an attempt to control such confounding relationships?	
What kind of population do the cases represent? Are they a heterogeneous representation of the disease or outcome being studied or a highly selected population for whom the responses may have limited generalizability?	
Are other biases evident? Is more known about the cases because they have received closer surveillance, volunteered more information, been subjected to more tests than the control group?	
Comments:	

(Adapted from material produced by the NHS Centre for Reviews and Dissemination. See Resources)

Figure A.7 Critical appraisal tool for case series	
Case series	
Author/s:	
Title of paper:	
Date:	
Outcomes measured:	
Principal outcomes:	
Is the study based on a random sample selected from a suitable sampling frame?	
Is there any evidence that the sample is representative of standard users of the intervention?	
Are the criteria for inclusion in the sample clearly defined?	
Did all individuals enter the survey at a similar point in their disease progression?	
Was follow-up long enough for important events to occur?	
Were outcomes assessed using objective criteria?	
If comparisons of series are being made, was there sufficient description of the series and the distribution of prognostic factors?	

(Adapted from material produced by the NHS Centre for Reviews and Dissemination. See Resources)

Various papers in this book were critically appraised. Papers whose quality was critically assessed were those that had met the inclusion criteria described under the heading Criteria for considering papers and addressed a specific research question with the most robust research methodology. Papers on adolescent suicide were not included in the critical appraisal. The type of critical appraisal tool used will be dictated by the types of study that are identified by the literature search. In the present publication only critical appraisal tools relating to systematic reviews/meta-analyses, such as the systematic review carried out by Hawton *et al.* (1998, 2001) on the efficacy of psychosocial and pharmacological treatments in preventing repetition (see Table A.8) and case-control studies, such as the case-control study carried out by Renaud *et al.* (1999) (see Table A.9) were employed.

Table A.8 Completed critical appraisal tool for the systematic review carried out by Hawton *et al.* (1998, 2001)

Systematic reviews/meta-analyses	
Author/s:	Hawton, Arensman, Townsend, Bremner, Feldman, Goldney, Gunnell, Hazell, van Heeringen, House, Owens, Sakinofsky and Traskman-Bendz.
Title of paper:	'Deliberate self-harm: Systematic review of efficacy of psychosocial and pharmacological treatments in preventing repetition.'
Date:	1998, 2001
Design:	Systematic review of 23 trials that were identified. Psychosocial and/or psychopharmacological treatment versus standard or less intensive types of aftercare.
Outcomes measured:	Repetition of deliberate self-harm.
Principal outcomes:	There is still uncertainty about which forms of psychosocial and physical treatments of self-harm patients are most effective. Larger trials of treatments associated with trends towards reduced rates of repetition of deliberate self-harm.
Are the results valid?	
Is the question clearly focused?	Clearly focused question stating that it is a systematic review of randomized controlled trials of psychosocial and physical treatments in preventing repetition of deliberate self-harm. The authors are less clear about the population that they are interested in, however.
Is the search thorough?	The search included Medline (1966–1996), PsychINFO (1974–1996), Embase (1980–1996) and the Cochrane Controlled Trials Register. Ten journals were also hand searched within the disciplines of psychology and psychiatry and all English journals concerned with suicide. However, the grey literature was not searched. Inclusion criteria seemed appropriate and the authors' attempt to gain additional information on standard aftercare where details are not provided.
Is the validity of included studies adequately assessed?	All studies included were randomized controlled trials. The quality of papers was rated by two independent reviewers, who were blind to authorship. The method of rating used was the quality of concealment of allocation, as recommended by Cochrane. The reviewers attempted to gain missing information from the authors. All reports had been published, but two studies had not been published in full; one was obtained from the author (an unpublished manuscript) and others were published conference proceedings.

Continued on next page

Table A.8 continued

What are the results?	
How big is the overall effect?	The overall effect was measured by calculating an odds ratio. No overall effect size is given – studies are divided into the type of treatment given.
Are the results consistent from study to study?	Generally, results of studies within each group were consistent between themselves. Sensitivity analyses, for example omitting trials, did not alter the results. Results therefore seem quite robust.
If the results of the review have been combined, was it reasonable to do so?	Having divided the studies into the four groups, it seems reasonable to have combined results in each group. Results are clearly displayed and variations in results are discussed and reasons given.
How precise are the results?	95% confidence interval used.
Interpretation of the results – Will they help in making decisions about patients?	
Do conclusions flow from evidence that is reviewed?	The conclusion that there is insufficient evidence to make firm recommendations about the most effective form of treatment do follow from the evidence presented.
Are sub-groups' analyses interpreted cautiously?	No sub-group analyses are presented.
Can the conclusions and data be generalized to other settings?	The studies included patients with a variety of presenting symptoms, so the results should be of relevance to a large number of patients who deliberately harm themselves and need treating in the community.
Were all important outcomes considered?	The review only focuses on repetition of deliberate self-harm. Other outcomes that may be of interest include other psychiatric diagnoses such as depression, problem resolution etc.
Are the benefits worth the harms and the costs?	The authors present no cost/risk benefit analysis. They state that more research is needed: 'large trials are required for the interventions shown in small trials to be of possible benefit'.
Comments:	The systematic review was carried out in order to examine the effectiveness of treatments of patients who have deliberately harmed themselves. Results overall seem to indicate that there is insufficient evidence to make any firm recommendations about which treatment intervention is most effective in reducing repetition of self-harming behaviour. Although promising results were found in individual studies for problem-solving therapy, dialectical behaviour therapy, depot neuroleptic medication and assertive outreach, further research is needed.

Table A.9 Completed critical appraisal tool for the case-control study carried out by Renaud *et al*. (1999)

Case-control studies	
Author:	Renaud, Brent, Birmaher, Chiappetta and Bridge.
Title of paper:	'Suicide in adolescents with disruptive disorders.'
Date:	1999
Design:	Case-control study.
Outcomes measured:	Demographic characteristics, details of the suicide, disruptive disorder details, comorbid psychiatric disorders, past suicidal behaviour and ideation, life events, family history of psychiatric disorder.
Principal outcomes:	Adolescents with disruptive disorders are at risk for suicide when comorbid substance abuse and a past history of suicide are present.
Is the information from the past dependable? Are data available from well-documented medical records with data recorded in a reliable method?	It is unclear how cases were identified and from where. Information was obtained through interviewing, so recall bias may be operating and information recalled may be limited.
If data has been recorded based on the recollection of subjects, is recall bias operating? What attempts have the authors made to assess the effect of this potential bias?	The authors have used multiple informants in order to try and obtain some sort of consensus on information obtained.
How alike are the control group? Are they really from a similar population differing only in the absence of disease?	The control group consisted of individuals from the community with disruptive disorder who had not committed suicide. Controls were of a similar age, race, gender, socio-economic status and country of residence.
Are there any other differences that might have a bearing on the outcome being studied? Have matching techniques been used in an attempt to control such confounding relationships?	A number of other variables were investigated including, demographic characteristics, characteristics of the suicide, characteristics of the disruptive disorders, psychiatric disorders, past suicidal behaviour, firearms, life events and family history of psychiatric disorder.
What kind of population do the cases represent? Are they a heterogeneous representation of the disease or outcome being studied or a highly selected population for whom the responses may have limited generalizability?	It is unclear as to what kind of population the cases represent as little detail is given about how subjects were recruited and where from. However, the majority of the population were white males, limiting generalizability.

Continued on next page

Table A.9 continued

Are other biases evident? Is more known about the cases because they have received closer surveillance, volunteered more information, been subjected to more tests than the control group?	No.
Comments:	The study has a relatively small sample size, which was almost entirely made up of males of white ethnic origin. However, multiple informants were used in order to combat recall bias and controls were similar on a number of important factors and taken from the same community.

References

Achenbach, T., Howell, C., McConaughy, S. and Stanger, C. (1995) 'Six-year predictions of problems in a national sample of children and youth: II. Signs of disturbance.' *Journal of the American Academy of Child and Adolescent Psychiatry 34*, 488–98.

Allard, R., Marshall, M. and Plante, M. (1992) 'Intensive follow-up does not decrease the risk of repeat suicide attempts.' *Suicide and Life-Threatening Behaviour 22*, 303–14.

American Psychiatric Association (2000) *Diagnostic and Statistical Manual of Mental Disorders (4th ed) Revised Text.* Washington, DC: American Psychiatric Association.

Anderson, J. and Larzelere, R. (1997) *Interim Summary of the Child Suicide Assessment.* Residential Research Technical Report #97–2, Boys Town, Boys Town, NE.

Andrews, J. and Lewinsohn, P. (1992) 'Suicidal attempts among older adolescents: Prevalence and co-occurrence with psychiatric disorders.' *Journal of the American Academy of Child and Adolescent Psychiatry 31*, 655–62.

Apsler, R. and Hodas, M. (1976) 'Evaluating hotlines with simulated calls.' *Crisis Intervention 6*, 14–21.

Apter, A., Bleich, A., Plutchik, R., Mendelsohn, S. and Tyano, S. (1988) 'Suicidal behaviour, depression and conduct disorder in hospitalised adolescents.' *Journal of the American Academy of Child and Adolescent Psychiatry 27*, 696–9.

Bancroft, J., Skrimshire, A., Casson, J., Harvard-Watts, O. and Reynolds, F. (1977) 'People who deliberately poison or injure themselves: Their problems and their contacts with helping agencies.' *Psychological Medicine 7*, 289–303.

Beautrais, A.L. (1998) *Risk Factors for Suicide and Attempted Suicide Amongst Young People.* A literature review prepared for the National Health and Medical Research Council.

Beautrais, A., Joyce, P. and Mulder, R. (1998) 'Psychiatric illness in a New Zealand sample of young people making serious suicide attempts.' *New Zealand Medical Journal 27*, 44–48.

Beck, A., Rush, A., Shaw, B. and Emery, G. (1979) *Cognitive Therapy of Depression.* New York: Guilford Press.

Beck, A., Schuyler, D. and Herman, I. (1974a) 'Development of suicidal intent scales.' In A. Beck, H. Resnik and D. Lettieri (eds) *The Prediction of Suicide.* Philadelphia: Charles Press.

Beck, A. and Steer, R. (1988) *Beck Hopelessness Scale Manual.* San Antonio: The Psychological Corporation.

Beck, A., Weissman, A., Lester, D. and Trexler, L. (1974b) 'The measurement of pessimism: The hopelessness scale.' *Journal of Consulting and Clinical Psychology 42*, 861, 865.

Birtchnell, J. and Alarcon, J. (1971) 'The motivation and emotional state of 91 cases of attempted suicide.' *British Journal of Medical Psychology 44*, 45–52.

Bleach, B. and Clairborn, W. (1974) 'Initial evaluation of hot-line telephone crisis centers.' *Community Mental Health Journal 10*, 387–94.

Boergers, J., Spirito, A. and Donaldson, D. (1998) 'Reasons for adolescent suicide attempts: Associations with psychological functioning.' *Journal of the American Academy of Child and Adolescent Psychiatry 37*, 1287–93.

Brent, D. (1997) 'Practitioner review: The aftercare of adolescents with deliberate self-harm.' *Journal of Child Psychology and Psychiatry 38*, 277–86.

Brent, D., Holder, D., Kolko, D., Birmaher, B., Baugher, M., Roth, C., Iyengar, S. and Johnson, B. (1997) 'A clinical psychotherapy trial for adolescent depression comparing cognitive, family and supportive treatments.' *Archives of General Psychiatry 54*, 877–85.

Brent, D., Kolko, D., Birmaher, B., Baugher, M., Bridge, J., Roth, C. and Holder, D. (1998c) 'Predictors of treatment efficacy in a clinical trial of three psychosocial treatments for adolescent depression.' *Journal of the American Academy of Child and Adolescent Psychiatry 37*, 906–14.

Brent, D., Kolko, D., Wartella, M., Boylan, M., Mortiz, G., Baugher, M. and Zelenak, J. (1993a) 'Adolescent psychiatric inpatients' risk of suicide attempt at 6-month follow-up.' *Journal of the American Academy of Child and Adolescent Psychiatry 32*, 95–105.

Brent, D., Perper, J., Goldstein, C., Kolko, D., Allan, M., Allman, C. and Zelenak, J. (1988a) 'Risk factors for adolescent suicide: A comparison of adolescent suicide victims with suicidal inpatients.' *Archives of General Psychiatry 45*, 581–8.

Brent, D., Perper, J., Kolko, D. and Zelenak, J. (1988b) 'The psychological autopsy: Methodological considerations for the study of adolescent suicide.' *Journal of the American Academy of Child and Adolescent Psychiatry 27*, 362–6.

Brent, D., Perper, J., Moritz, G., Allman, C., Friend, A., Roth, C., Schweers, J., Balach, L. and Baugher, M. (1993b) 'Psychiatric risk factors for adolescent suicide: A case-control study.' *Journal of the American Academy of Child and Adolescent Psychiatry 32*, 521–9.

Brent, D., Perper, J., Moritz, G., Allman, C., Roth, C., Schweers, J. and Balach, L. (1993c) 'The validity of diagnoses obtained through the psychological autopsy procedure in adolescent suicide victims: Use of family history.' *Acta Psychiatrica Scandinavica 87*, 118–22.

Bridge, T., Potkin, S., Zung, W. and Soldo, B. (1977) 'Suicide prevention centres: Ecological study of effectiveness.' *The Journal of Nervous and Mental Diseases 164*, 18–24.

Burgess, S., Hawton, K. and Loveday, G. (1998) 'Adolescents who take overdoses: Outcome in terms of changes in psychopathology and the adolescents' attitudes to care and to their overdose.' *Journal of Adolescence 21, 209–18.*

Cappelli, M., Clulow, M., Goodman, J., Davidson, S., Feder, S., Baron, P., Manion, I. and McGrath, P. (1995) 'Identifying depressed and suicidal adolescents in a teen health clinic.' *Journal of Adolescent Health 16*, 64–70.

Catalan, J., Marsack, P., Hawton, K., Whitwell, D., Fagg, J. and Bancroft, J. (1980) 'Comparison of doctors and nurses in the assessment of deliberate self-poisoning patients.' *Psychological Medicine 10*, 483–91.

Cavaiola, A. and Lavender, N. (1999) 'Suicidal behaviour in chemically dependent adolescents.' *Adolescence 34*, 735–44.

Charlton, J., Kelly, S. and Dunnell, K. (1993) *Suicide Deaths in England and Wales: Trends in Factors Associated with Suicide Deaths.* Population Trends 71, 34–42. ONS, London: HMSO.

Choquet, M. and Ledoux, S. (1994) *Adolescents: Enquête Nationale.* Villejuif Cedex: Inserm.

Choquet, M. and Menke, H. (1990) 'Suicidal thoughts during early adolescence: Prevalence, associated troubles and help-seeking behaviour.' *Acta Psychiatrica Scandinavica 81*, 170–7.

Clark, D. (1993) 'Suicidal behaviour in childhood and adolescence: Recent studies and clinical implications.' *Psychiatric Annals 23*, 271–83.

The Cochrane Collaboration (1996) *Cochrane Collaboration Handbook.* Oxford: The Cochrane Collaboration.

Cole, D. (1989a) 'Psychopathology or adolescent suicide: Hopelessness, coping beliefs and depression.' *Journal of Abnormal Psychology 98*, 248–55.

Cole, D. (1989b) 'Validation of the reasons for living inventory in general and delinquent adolescent samples.' *Journal of Abnormal Child Psychology 17*, 13–26.

Cotgrove, A., Zirinsky, L., Black, D. and Weston, D. (1995) 'Secondary prevention of attempted suicide in adolescence.' *Journal of Adolescence 18*, 569–77.

Crawford, M. and Wessely, S. (1998) 'Does initial management affect the rate of repetition of deliberate self-harm? Cohort study.' *British Medical Journal 15*, 18–22.

Cull, J. and Gill, W. (1988) *Suicide Probability Scale (SPS) Manual.* Los Angeles: Western Psychological Services.

Cummings, P., Grosman, D., Rivara, F. and Koepsell, T. (1997) 'State gun safe storage laws and child mortality due to firearms.' *Journal of the American Medical Association 278*, 1084–6.

D'Attilio, J., Campbell, B., Lubold, P., Jacobson, T. and Richard, J. (1992) 'Social support and suicide potential: Preliminary findings for adolescent populations.' *Psychological Reports 70*, 76–8.

De Moore, G. and Robertson, A. (1996) 'Suicide in the 18 years after deliberate self-harm. A prospective study.' *British Journal of Psychiatry 169*, 489–94.

Department of Health and Social Security (1984) *The Management of Deliberate Self-harm. HN(84)25.* London: Department of Health and Social Security.

de Wilde, E., Kienhorst, I., Diekstra, R. and Wolters, W. (1993) 'The specificity of psychological characteristics of adolescent suicide attempters.' *Journal of the American Child and Adolescent Psychiatry 32*, 51–9.

Dew, M., Bromet, E., Brent, D. and Greenhouse, J. (1987) 'A quantitative literature review of the effectiveness of suicide prevention centres.' *Journal of Consulting and Clinical Psychology 55*, 239–44.

Deykin, E., Chung-Chen, H., Joshi, N. and McNamarra, J. (1986) 'Adolescent suicidal and self-destructive behaviour: Results of an intervention study.' *Journal of Adolescent Health Care 7*, 88–95.

Diekstra, R. (1974) 'A social learning approach to the prediction of suicidal behaviour.' In N. Speyer, R. Diekstra and K. van de Loo (eds) *Proceedings of the 7th International Conference for Suicide Prevention, Amsterdam, August 27–30, 1973.* Amsterdam: Swets and Zeitlinger.

Diekstra, R. and Garnefski, N. (1995) 'On the nature, magnitude and causality of suicidal behaviours: An international perspective.' *Suicide and Life-Threatening Behaviour 25*, 36–57.

Diekstra, R., Kienhorst, C. and Wilds, E. (1995) 'Suicide and suicidal behaviour among adolescents.' In M. Rutter and D. Smith (eds) *Psychosocial Disorders in Young People: Time Trends and their Causes.* Chichester: Wiley.

Dinges, N. and Duong-Tran, Q. (1994) 'Suicide ideation and suicide attempt among American Indian and Alaska native boarding school adolescents.' *American Indian and Alaskan Native Mental Health Research Monograph Series 4*, 168–88.

Donaldson, D., Spirito, A., Arigan, M. and Aspel, J. (1997) 'Structured disposition planning for adolescent suicide attempters in a general hospital: Preliminary findings on short-term outcome.' *Archives of Suicide Research 3*, 271–82.

Dubow, E., Kausch, D., Blum, M., Reed, J. and Bush, E. (1989) 'Correlates of suicidal ideation and attempts in a community sample of junior high and high school students.' *Journal of Clinical Child Psychology 18*, 158–66.

Dyck, R. (1994) 'Guidelines for the development and organisation of suicide prevention programs.' In R. Diekstra and W. Gulbinat (eds) *Preventive Strategies on Suicide.* Canberra/Leiden: Brill.

Eggert, L., Thompson, E. and Herting, J. (1994) 'A measure of adolescent potential for suicide (MAPS): Development and preliminary findings.' *Suicide and Life-Threatening Behaviour 24*, 359–81.

Enns, M., Inayatulla, M., Cox, B. and Cheyne, L. (1997) 'Prediction of suicide intent in Aboriginal and non-Aboriginal adolescent inpatients: A research note.' *Suicide and Life-Threatening Behaviour 27*, 218–24.

Feldman, M. and Wilson, A. (1997) 'Adolescent suicidality in urban minorities and its relationship to conduct disorders, depression, and separation anxiety.' *Journal of the American Academy of Child and Adolescent Psychiatry 36*, 75–84.

Firestone, R. and Firestone, L. (1998) 'Voices in suicide: The relationship between self-destructive thought processes, maladaptive behaviour and self-destructive manifestations.' *Death Studies 22*, 411–33.

Freud, S. (1917) *Mourning and Melancholia, Standard Edition, Vol 14.* London: Hogarth.

Gardner, R., Hanka, R., Evison, B., Mountford, P., O'Brien, V. and Roberts, S. (1978) 'Consultation-liaison scheme for self-poisoned patients in a general hospital.' *British Medical Journal 2*, 1392–4.

Garland, A., Shaffer, D. and Whittle, B. (1989) 'A national survey of school-based, adolescent suicide prevention programs.' *Journal of the American Academy of Child and Adolescent Psychiatry 28*, 931–4.

Garland, A. and Zigler, E. (1993) 'Adolescent suicide prevention: Current research and social policy implications.' *American Psychologist 48*, 169–82.

Garnefski, N. and Diekstra, R. (1995) 'Suicidal behaviour and the co-occurrence of behavioural, emotional and cognitive problems among adolescents.' *Archives of Suicide Research 1*, 243–60.

Garnefski, N., Diekstra, R. and de Heus, P. (1992) 'A population-based survey of the characteristics of high school students with and without a history of suicidal behaviour.' *Acta Psychiatrica Scandinavica 86*, 189–96.

Garrison, C. (1989) 'The study of suicidal behaviour in schools.' *Suicide and Life -Threatening Behaviour 19*, 120–30.

Garrison, C., Addy, C., Jackson, K., McKeown, R. and Waller, J. (1991) 'A longitudinal study of suicidal ideation in young adolescents.' *Journal of the American Academy of Child and Adolescent Psychiatry 30*, 597–603.

Gilbody, S., House, A. and Owens, D. (1997) 'The early repetition of deliberate self-harm.' *Journal of the Royal College of Physicians London 31*, 171–2.

Goldacre, M. and Hawton, K. (1985) 'Repetition of self-poisoning and subsequent death in adolescents who take overdoses.' *British Journal of Psychiatry 146*, 395–8.

Goldberg, D. (1978) *General Health Questionnaire.* Windsor: NFER-Nelson.

Goldston, D., Daniel, D., Revoussin, B., Reboussin, D. and Frazier, P. (2000) 'Cognitive risk factors and suicide attempts among formerly hospitalised adolescents: A prospective naturalistic study.' *Journal of the American Academy of Child and Adolescent Psychiatry 40*, 91–9.

Goldston, D. (2000) *Assessment of Suicidal Behaviours and Risk Among Children and Adolescents.* Technical report submitted to NIMH under contract no. 263-MD-909995.

Gould, M., King, R., Greenwald, S., Fisher, P., Schwab-Stone, M., Kramer, R., Flisher, A., Goodman, S., Canino, G. and Shaffer, D. (1998) 'Psychopathology associated with suicidal ideation and attempts among children and adolescents.' *Journal of the American Academy of Child and Adolescent Psychiatry 37*, 915–23.

Gutierrez, P., Osman, A., Kopper, B. and Barrios, F. (2000) 'Why young people do not kill themselves: The reasons for living inventory for adolescents.' *Journal of Clinical Child Psychology 29*, 177–87.

Haldane, J. and Haider, I. (1967) 'Attempted suicide in children and adolescents.' *British Journal of Clinical Practice 21*, 587–91.

Hansburg, H. (1980a) *Adolescent Separation Anxiety Test.* Melbourne, FL: Krieger.

Hansburg, H. (1980b) *Adolescent Separation Anxiety: A Method for the Study of Adolescent Separation Problems, Vols 1–2.* Melbourne, FL: Krieger.

Harrington, R., Kerfoot, M., Dyer, E., McNiven, F., Gill, J., Harrington, V. and Woodham, A. (2000) 'Deliberate self-poisoning in adolescence: Why does a brief family intervention work in some cases and not others?' *Journal of Adolescence 23*, 13–20.

Harrington, R., Kerfoot, M., Dyer, E., McNiven, F., Gill, J., Harrington, V., Woodham, A. and Byford, S. (1998) 'Randomized trial of a home-based family intervention for children who have deliberately poisoned themselves.' *Journal of the American Academy of Child and Adolescent Psychiatry 37*, 512–18.

Hassan, R. (1995) 'Effects of newspaper stories on the incidence of suicide in Australia: A research note.' *Australian and New Zealand Journal of Psychiatry 29*, 480–3.

Hawton, K. (1986) *Suicide and Attempted Suicide among Children and Adolescents.* Beverley Hills: Sage.

Hawton, K. (1996) 'Suicide and attempted suicide in young people.' In A. McFarlane (ed) *Adolescent Medicine.* London: Royal College of Physicians.

Hawton, K., Arensman, E., Townsend, E., Bremner, S., Feldman, E., Goldney, R., Gunnell, D., Hazell, P. and van Heeringen, K. (1998) 'Deliberate self harm: Systematic review of efficacy of psychosocial and pharmacological treatments in preventing repetition.' *British Medical Journal 317*, 441–7.

Hawton, K., Bancroft, J., Catalan, J., Kingston, B., Stedeford, A. and Welch, N. (1981) 'Domiciliary and out-patient treatment of self-poisoning patients by medical and non-medical staff.' *Psychological Medicine 11*, 169–77.

Hawton, K. and Catalan, J. (1987) *Attempted Suicide. A Practical Guide to its Nature and Management (2nd ed).* Oxford: Oxford University Press.

Hawton, K., Cole, D., O'Grady, J. and Osborn, M. (1982b) 'Motivational aspects of deliberate self-poisoning in adolescents.' *British Journal of Psychiatry 141*, 286–91.

Hawton, K. and Fagg, J. (1988) 'Suicide and other causes of death following attempted suicide.' *British Journal of Psychiatry 152*, 259–66.

Hawton, K. and Fagg, J. (1992) 'Deliberate self-poisoning and self-injury in adolescents: A study of characteristics and trends in Oxford, 1976–1989.' *British Journal of Psychiatry 161*, 816–23.

Hawton, K., Fagg, J., Platt, S. and Hawkins, M. (1993) 'Factors associated with suicide after parasuicide in young people.' *British Medical Journal 306*, 1641–4.

Hawton, K., Fagg, J., Simkin, S., Bale, B. and Bond, A. (1997) 'Trends in deliberate self-harm in Oxford, 1985–1995.' *British Journal of Psychiatry 171*, 556–60.

Hawton, K., Fagg, J., Simkin, S., Bale, B. and Bond, A. (2000) 'Deliberate self-harm in adolescents in Oxford, 1985–1995.' *Journal of Adolescence 23*, 47–55.

Hawton, K. and Goldacre, M. (1982) 'Hospital admissions for adverse effects of medicinal agents (mainly self-poisoning) among adolescents in the Oxford region.' *British Journal of Psychiatry 141*, 166–70.

Hawton, K., Kingsbury, S., Steinhardt, K., James, A. and Fagg, J. (1999) 'Repetition of deliberate self-harm by adolescents: The role of psychological factors.' *Journal of Adolescence 22*, 369–78.

Hawton, K., O'Grady, J., Osborn, M. and Cole, D. (1982a) 'Adolescents who take overdoses: Their characteristics, problems and contacts with helping agencies.' *British Journal of Psychiatry 140*, 118–23.

Hawton, K., Osborn, M., O'Grady, J. and Cole, D. (1982c) 'Classification of adolescents who take overdoses.' *British Journal of Psychiatry 140*, 124–31.

Hawton, K., Rodham, K., Evans, E. and Weatherall, R. (2002) 'Deliberate self harm in adolescents: Self report survey in schools in England.' *British Medical Journal 325*, 1207–11.

Hawton, K., Townsend, E., Arensman, E., Gunnell, D., Hazell, P., House, A. and van Heeringen, K. (2001) 'Psychosocial and pharmacological treatments for deliberate self-harm.' *Cochrane Review 1*. Oxford: Software Update.

Hawton, K. and van Heeringen, K. (eds) (2000) *The International Handbook of Suicide and Attempted Suicide.* Chichester: Wiley.

Hawton, K. and Williams, K. (2001) 'The connection between media and suicidal behaviour warrants serious attention.' *Crisis 22*, 137–40.

Hazell, P., O'Conell, D., Heathcote, D., Robertson, J. and Henry, D. (1995) 'Efficacy of trycyclic drugs in treating child and adolescent depression: A meta-analysis.' *British Medical Journal 310*, 897–901.

Hewitt, P., Newton, J., Flett, G. and Callander, L. (1997) 'Perfectionism and suicide ideation in adolescent psychiatric patients.' *Journal of Abnormal Child Psychology 25*, 95–101.

Hiatt, M. and Cornell, D. (1999) 'Concurrent validity of the Millon adolescent clinical inventory as a measure of depression in hospitalised adolescents.' *Journal of Personality Assessment 73*, 64–79.

Hills, N. (1995) 'Newspaper stories and the incidence of suicide.' *Australian and New Zealand Journal of Psychiatry 29*, 699.

Hoberman, H. and Garfinkel, B. (1988) 'Completed suicide in children and adolescents.' *Journal of the American Academy of Child and Adolescent Psychiatry 27*, 689–95.

Hollis, C. (1996) 'Depression, family environment and adolescent suicidal behaviour.' *Journal of the American Academy of Child and Adolescent Psychiatry 35*, 622–30.

Houston, K., Hawton, K. and Shepperd, R. (2001) 'Suicide in young people aged 15–24: A psychological autopsy study.' *Journal of Affective Disorders 63*, 159–70.

Humphry, D. (2002) *Final Exit: The Practicalities of Self-Deliverance and Assisted Suicide for the Dying.* 3rd ed. Oregan: Delta.

Ivanoff, A., Jang, S., Smyth, N. and Linehan, M. (1994) 'Fewer reasons for staying alive when you are thinking of killing yourself: The brief reasons for living inventory.' *Journal of Psychopathology and Behavioural Assessment 16*, 1–13.

Jonas, K. (1992) 'Modelling and suicide. A test of the Werther effect.' *British Journal of Social Psychology 31*, 295–306.

Jones, G. (1997) 'The role of drugs and alcohol in urban minority adolescent suicide attempts.' *Death Studies 21*, 189–202.

Kann, L., Kinchen, S., Williams, B., Ross, J., Lowry, R. and Grunbaum, J. (2000) 'Youth risk behaviour surveillance – United States 1999.' *MMWR Morb Mortal Weekly Report 49*, 1–96.

Kaplan, S., Pelcovitz, D., Salzinger, S., Mandel, F. and Weiner, M. (1997) 'Adolescent physical abuse and suicide attempts.' *Journal of the American Academy of Child and Adolescent Psychiatry 36*, 799–808.

Kashani, J., Soltys, S., Dandoy, A., Vaidya, A. and Reid, J. (1991) 'Correlates of hopelessness in psychiatrically hospitalised children.' *Comprehensive Psychiatry 32*, 330–7.

Kashden, J., Fremouw, W., Callahan, T. and Franzen, M. (1993) 'Impulsivity in suicidal and non-suicidal adolescents.' *Journal of Abnormal Child Psychology 21*, 339–53.

Kazdin, A., French, N., Unis, A., Esveldt-Dawson, D. and Sherick, R. (1983) 'Hopelessness, depression and suicidal intent among psychiatrically disturbed inpatient children.' *Journal of Consulting and Clinical Psychology 51*, 504–10.

Kazdin, A., Rodgers, A. and Colbus, D. (1986) 'The hopelessness scale for children: Psychometric characteristics and concurrent validity.' *Journal of Consulting and Clinical Psychology 54*, 241–5.

Kerfoot, M. (1988) 'Deliberate self-poisoning in childhood and early adolescence.' *Journal of Child Psychology and Psychiatry 29*, 335–43.

Kerfoot, M. (1996) 'Suicide and deliberate self-harm in children and adolescents: A research update.' *Children and Society 10*, 236–41.

Kerfoot, M., Dyer, E., Harrington, V., Woodham, A. and Harrington, R. (1996) 'Correlates and short-term course of self-poisoning in adolescents.' *British Journal of Psychiatry 168*, 38–42.

Kessler, R., Downey, G. and Stipp, H. (1998) 'Clustering of teenage suicide after television news stories about suicide: A reconsideration' *American Journal of Psychiatry 145,* 1379-883.

Kienhorst, C., De Wilde, E., Van den Bout, J., Diekstra, R. and Wolters, W. (1990a) 'Self-reported suicidal behaviour in Dutch secondary education students.' *Suicide and Life Threatening Behaviour 20*, 101–112.

Kienhorst, C., De Wilde, E., Van den Bout, J., Diekstra, R. and Wolters, W. (1990b) 'Characteristics of suicide attempters in a population-based sample of Dutch adolescents.' *British Journal of Psychiatry 156*, 243–248.

King, J. and Kowalchuck, B. (1994) *Manual for ISO-30 Adolescent: Inventory of Suicide Orientation-30.* Minneapolis: National Computer Systems.

Kingsbury, S. (1996) 'PATHOS: A screening instrument for adolescent overdose: A research note.' *Journal of Child Psychology and Psychiatry 37*, 609–11.

Kingsbury, S., Hawton, K., Steinhardt, D. and James, A. (1999) 'Do adolescents who take overdoses have specific psychological characteristics? A comparative study with psychiatric and community controls.' *Journal of the American Academy of Child and Adolescent Psychiatry 38*, 1125–31.

Kovacs, M. (1982) *Children's Depression Inventory.* Pittsburgh: Western Psychiatric Institute and Clinic.

Kovacs, M. and Beck, A. (1977) 'An empirical clinical approach towards a definition of childhood depression.' In J. Schulterbrandt and A. Raskin (eds) *Depression in Children.* New York: Raven Press.

Kovacs, M., Goldston, D. and Gatsonis, C. (1993) 'Suicidal behaviours and childhood-onset depressive disorders: A longitudinal investigation.' *Journal of the American Academy of Child and Adolescent Psychiatry 32*, 8–20.

Kreitman, N. (1977) *Parasuicide.* London: Wiley.

Kreitman, N., Smith, P. and Tan, E. (1970) 'Attempted suicide as language: An empirical study.' *British Journal of Psychiatry 116*, 465–73.

Larzelere, R. and Andersen, J. (1998) Child Suicide Assessment. Unpublished Instrument. Father Flanagan's Boys Home, Boys Town, NE.

Larzelere, R., Smith, G., Batenhorst, L. and Kelly, D. (1996) 'Predictive validity of the suicide probability scale among adolescents in group home treatment.' *Journal of the American Academy of Child and Adolescent Psychiatry 35*, 166–72.

Leon, A., Friedman, R., Sweeney, J., Brown, R. and Mann, J. (1990) 'Statistical issues in the identification of risk factors for suicidal behaviour: The application of survival analysis.' *Psychiatry Residents 31*, 99–108.

Lester, D. (1972) *Why People Kill Themselves: A Summary of Research Findings on Suicidal Behaviour.* Springfield: Thomas.

Lewinsohn, P., Langhinrichsen-Rohling, J., Langford, R., Rohde, P., Seeley, J. and Chapman, J. (1995) 'The life attitudes schedule: A scale to assess adolescent life-enhancing and life-threatening behaviours.' *Suicide and Life-Threatening Behaviour 25*, 458–74.

Lewinsohn, P., Rohde, P. and Seeley, J. (1993) 'Psychosocial characteristics of adolescents with a history of suicide attempt.' *Journal of the American Academy of Child and Adolescent Psychiatry 32*, 60–8.

Lewinsohn, P., Rohde, P. and Seeley, J. (1994) 'Psychosocial risk factors for future adolescent suicide attempts.' *Journal of Consulting and Clinical Psychology 62*, 297–305.

Lewis, S., Johnson, J., Cohen, P., Garcia, M. and Velez, C. (1988) 'Attempted suicide in youth: Its relationship to school achievement, education goals and socio-economic status.' *Journal of Abnormal Child Psychology 16*, 459–71.

Linehan, M., Goodstein, J., Nielsen, S. and Chiles, J. (1983) 'Reasons for staying alive when you are thinking of killing yourself: The reasons for living inventory.' *Journal of Consulting and Clinical Psychology 51*, 276–86.

Marciano, P. and Kazdin, A. (1994) 'Self-esteem, depression, hopelessness and suicidal intent among psychiatrically disturbed inpatient children.' *Journal of Clinical Child Psychology 23*, 151–60.

Martin, G. (1996) 'The influence of television suicide in a normal adolescent population.' *Archives of Suicide Research 2*, 103–17.

Marttunen, M., Aro, H., Henriksson, M. and Lonnqvist, J. (1991) 'Mental disorders in adolescent suicide: DSM-III-R axes I and II diagnoses in suicides among 13–19 year olds in Finland.' *Archives of General Psychiatry 48*, 834–9.

Marttunen, M., Aro, H. and Lonnqvist, J. (1993) 'Precipitant stressors in adolescent suicide.' *Journal of the American Academy of Child and Adolescent Psychiatry 32*, 1178–83.

Marzuk, P., Tardiff, D., Hirsch, C., Leon, A., Stajic, M., Hartwell, N. and Portera, L. (1993) 'Increase in suicide by asphyxiation in New York City after the publication of *Final Exit.*' *New England Journal of Medicine 329*, 1508–10.

Marzuk, P., Tardiff, D., Hirsch, C., Leon, A., Stajic, M., Hartwell, N. and Portera, L. (1994) 'Increase in suicide by asphyxiation in New York City after the publication of *Final Exit.*' *Publishing Research Quarterly 10*, 62–8.

McCleavy, B., Daly, J., Murray, C., O'Riordan, J. and Taylor, M. (1987) 'Interpersonal problem-solving deficits in self-poisoning patients.' *Suicide and Life-Threatening Behaviour 17*, 33–49.

Meltzer, H., Harrington, R., Goodman, R. and Jenkins, R. (2001) *Children and Adolescents who Try to Harm, Hurt or Kill Themselves.* Newport, UK: Office for National Statistics.

Mental Health Foundation (2000) 'Self-Harm Factsheet.' www.mentalhealth.org.uk.

Miller, H., Coombs, D., Leeper, J. and Barton, S. (1984) 'An analysis of the effects of suicide prevention facilities on suicide rates in the United States.' *American Journal of Public Health 74*, 340–3.

Miller, I., Epstein, N., Bishop, D. and Keitner, G. (1985) 'The McMaster family assessment device: Reliability and validity.' *Journal of Marital and Family Therapy 11*, 345–56.

Millon, T. (1993) *Millon Adolescent Clinical Inventory: Manual*. Minneapolis: National Computer Systems.

Ministry of Health (1961) *HM Circular (61), 94*. London: Ministry of Health.

Morgan, H., Jones, E. and Owen, J. (1993) 'Secondary prevention of non-fatal deliberate self-harm. The green card study.' *British Journal of Psychiatry 163*, 111–2.

Mulder, A., Methorst, G. and Diekstra, R. (1989) 'Prevention of suicidal behaviour in adolescents: The role and training of teachers.' *Crisis 10*, 36–51.

Myers, K., McCauley, E., Calderon, R. and Treder, R. (1991) 'The 3-year longitudinal course of suicidality and predictive factors for subsequent suicidality in youths with major depressive disorder.' *Journal of the American Academy of Child and Adolescent Psychiatry 30*, 804–10.

Newson-Smith, J. and Hirsch, S. (1979) 'A comparison of social workers and psychiatrists in evaluating parasuicide.' *British Journal of Psychiatry 134*, 335–42.

NHS Centre for Reviews and Dissemination (1996) 'Undertaking systematic reviews of research on effectiveness.' (CRD Guidelines for those carrying out or commissioning reviews, CRD Report 4). York: NHS Centre for Reviews and Dissemination.

NHS Centre for Reviews and Dissemination (1998) 'Deliberate self-harm.' *Effective Health Care 4*, December.

Orbach, I., Bar-Joseph, H. and Dror, N. (1990) 'Styles of problem solving in suicidal individuals.' *Suicide and Life-Threatening Behaviour 20*, 56–64.

Orbach, I., Lotem-Peleg, M. and Kedem, P. (1995) 'Attitudes toward the body in suicidal, depressed and normal adolescents.' *Suicide and Life-Threatening Behaviour 25*, 211–21.

Orbach, I., Mikulincer, M., Blumenson, R., Mester, R. and Stein, D. (1999) 'The subjective experience of problem irresolvability and suicidal behaviour: Dynamics and measurement.' *Suicide and Life-Threatening Behaviour 29*, 150–64.

Orbach, I., Milstein, I., Har-Even, D., Apter, A., Tiano, S. and Elizur, A. (1991) 'A multi-attitude suicide tendency scale for adolescents.' *Psychological Assessment 3*, 398–404.

Osman, A., Barrios, F., Panak, W., Osman, J., Hoffman, J. and Hammer, R. (1994) 'Validation of the multi-attitude suicide tendency scale in adolescent samples.' *Journal of Clinical Psychology 50*, 847–55.

Osman, A., Downs, W., Kopper, B., Barrios, F., Baker, M., Osman, J., Besett, T. and Linehan, M. (1998) 'The reasons for living inventory for adolescents (RFL-A): Development and psychometric properties.' *Journal of Clinical Psychology 54*, 1063–78.

Osman, A., Kopper, B., Barrios, F., Osman, J., Besett, F. and Linehan, M. (1996) 'The brief reasons for living inventory for adolescents (BRFL-A).' *Journal of Abnormal Child Psychology 24*, 433–43.

Ostroff, R., Behrends, R., Kinson, L. and Oliphant, J. (1985) 'Adolescent suicides modelled after television movie.' *American Journal of Psychiatry 142*, 989.

Otto, U. (1972) 'Suicidal acts by children and adolescents: A follow-up study.' *Acta Psychiatrica Scandinavica 233*, 7–123.

Owens, D., Horrocks, J. and House A. (2002) 'Fatal and non-fatal repetition of self-harm.' *British Journal of Psychiatry 181*, 193–99.

Pfeffer, C. (1992) 'Relationship between depression and suicidal behaviour.' In M. Shafii and S. Shafii (eds) *Clinical Guide to Depression in Children and Adolescents.* Washington: American Psychiatric Press.

Pfeffer, C., Conte, H., Plutchik, R. and Jerrett, I. (1979) 'Suicidal behaviour in latency-age children: An empirical study.' *Journal of the American Academy of Child and Adolescent Psychiatry 18,* 679–92.

Pfeffer, C., Klerman, G., Hurt, S., Kakuma, T., Peskin, J. and Siefker, C. (1993) 'Suicidal children grow up: Rates and psychosocial risk factors for suicidal attempts during follow-up.' *Journal of the American Academy of Child and Adolescent Psychiatry 32,* 106–13.

Pfeffer, C. Klerman, G., Hurt, S., Lesser, M., PeskinF. and Siefker, C. (1991) 'Suicidal children grow up: Demographic and clinical risk factors for adolescent suicide attempts.' *Journal of the American Academy of Child and Adolescent Psychiatry 30,* 609–616.

Pfeffer, C., Nercorn, J., Kaplan, G., Misruchi, M. and Plutchik, R. (1988) 'Subtypes of suicidal and assaultive behaviours in adolescent psychiatric in-patients: A research note.' *Journal of Child Psychology and Psychiatry 30,* 151–63.

Phillips, D. (1974) 'The influence of suggestion on suicide: Substantive and theoretical implications of the Werther effect.' *American Sociological Review 39,* 340–54.

Piersma, H. and Boes, J. (1997) 'Utility of the inventory of suicide orientation-30 (ISP-30) for adolescent psychiatric inpatients: Linking clinical decision making with outcome evaluation.' *Journal of Clinical Psychology 53,* 65–72.

Pinto, A., Whisman, M. and Conwell, Y. (1998) 'Reasons for living in a clinical sample of adolescents.' *Journal of Adolescence 21,* 397–405.

Pirkis, J. and Blood, R. (2001) *Suicide and the Media: A Critical Review.* Canberra: Commonwealth Department of Health and Aged Care.

Platt, S. (1993) 'The social transmission of parasuicide: Is there a modelling effect?' *Crisis 14,* 23–31.

Platt, S., Hawton, K., Kreitman, N., Fagg, J. and Foster, J. (1988) 'Recent clinical and epidemiological trends in parasuicide in Edinburgh and Oxford: A tale of two cities.' *Psychological Medicine 18,* 405–18.

Ploeg, J., Ciliska, D., Dobbins, M., Hayward, S., Thomas, H. and Underwood, J. (1996) 'A systematic overview of adolescent suicide prevention programs.' *Canadian Journal of Public Health 87,* 319–24.

Pronovost, J., Cote, L. and Ross, C. (1990) 'Epidemiological study of suicidal behaviour among secondary-school students.' *Canada's Mental Health 38,* 9–14.

Ramchandani, P., Joughin, C. and Zui, M. (2001) 'Evidence-based child and adolescent mental health services – oxymoron or brave new dawn?' *Child Psychology and Psychiatry Review 6,* 59–64.

Reifman, A. and Windle, M. (1995) 'Adolescent suicidal behaviours as a function of depression, hopelessness, alcohol use and social support: A longitudinal investigation.' *American Journal of Community Psychology 23,* 329–54.

Renaud, J., Brent, D., Birmaher, B., Chiappetta, L. and Bridge, J. (1999) 'Suicide in adolescents with disruptive disorders.' *Journal of the American Academy of Child and Adolescent Psychiatry 38,* 846–51.

Reynolds, W. (1988) *Suicidal Ideation Questionnaire. Professional Manual.* Odessa: Psychological Assessment Resources.

Rich, C., Sherman, M. and Fowler, R. (1990) 'San Diego suicide study: The adolescents.' *Adolescence 25,* 856–65.

Rich, C., Young, D. and Fowler, R. (1986) 'San Diego suicide study: I. young versus old subjects.' *Archives of General Psychiatry 43*, 577–82.

Richman, J. (1979) 'The family therapy of attempted suicide.' *Family Process 18*, 131–42.

Rohde, P., Lewinsohn, P., Seeley, J. and Langhinrichsen, J. (1996) 'The life attitudes schedule short form: An abbreviated measure of life-enhancing and life-threatening behaviours in adolescents.' *Suicide and Life-Threatening Behaviour 26*, 272–81.

Rotheram, M. (1987) 'Evaluation of imminent danger for suicide among youth.' *American Journal of Orthopsychiatry 57*, 102–10.

Rotheram-Borus, M., Piacentini, J., Miller, S., Graae, F., Dune, E. and Cantwell, C. (1996) 'Toward improving treatment adherence among adolescent suicide attempters.' *Clinical Child Psychology and Psychiatry 1*, 99–108.

Rotheram-Borus, M. and Trautman, P. (1990) 'Cognitive style and pleasant activities among female adolescent suicide attempters.' *Journal of Consulting and Clinical Psychology 58*, 554–61.

Royal College of Psychiatrists (1994) *The General Hospital Management of Adult Deliberate Self-harm. Council Report CR32.* London: Royal College of Psychiatrists.

Royal College of Psychiatrists (1998) *Managing Deliberate Self-Harm in Young People. Council Report CR64.* London: Royal College of Psychiatrists, Gaskell Publications.

Rubinstein, J., Heelen, T., Housman, D., Rubin, C. and Stechler, G. (1989) 'Suicidal behaviour in normal adolescents: Risk factors and protective factors.' *American Journal of Orthopsychiatry 59*, 59–71.

Sackett, D., Rosenberg, W., Gray, J., Haynes, R. and Richardson, W. (1996) 'Evidence based medicine: What it is and what it isn't.' *British Medical Journal 312*, 71–2.

Sadowski, C. and Kelly, M. (1993) 'Social problem solving in suicidal adolescents.' *Journal of Consulting and Clinical Psychology 61*, 121–7.

Safer, D. (1996) 'A comparison of studies from the United States and Western Europe on psychiatric hospitalisation referrals for youths exhibiting suicidal behaviour.' *Annals of Clinical Psychiatry 8*, 161–8.

Safer, D. (1997a) 'Adolescent/adult differences in suicidal behaviour and outcome.' *Annals of Clinical Psychiatry 9*, 61–6.

Safer, D. (1997b) 'Self-reported suicide attempts by adolescents.' *Annals of Clinical Psychiatry 9*, 263–9.

Salkovskis, P., Atha, C. and Storer, D. (1990) 'Cognitive-behavioural problem solving in the treatment of patients who repeatedly attempt suicide. A controlled trial.' *British Journal of Psychiatry 157*, 871–6.

Schmidtke, A. (1988) *Verhaltenstheoretisches Erklarungimodell Suizidalen Verhaltens.* Regensberg: Roderer.

Schmidtke, A. (1996) *Mass Media: Their Impact on Suicide among Adolescents.* Paper presented at the International Conference, 'Suicide: Biopsychosocial Approaches', Athens.

Schmidtke, A., Bille-Brahe, U., DeLeo, D., Kerkhof, A., Bjerke, T., Crepet, P., Haring, C., Hawton, K., Lonnqvist, J., Michel, K., Pommereau, X., Querejeta, I., Phillipe, I., Salander-Renberg, E., Temesvary, B., Wasserman, D., Fricke, S., Weinacker, B. and Sampaio-Faria, J. (1996) 'Attempted suicide in Europe: Rates, trends and sociodemographic characteristics of suicide attempters during the period 1989–1992. Results of the WHO/EURO multicentre study of parasuicide.' *Acta Psychiatrica Scandinavica 93*, 327–38.

Schmidtke, A. and Hafner, H. (1988) 'The Werther effect after television films: New evidence for an old hypothesis.' *Psychological Medicine 18*, 665–76.

Schmidtke, A. and Schaller, S. (1998) 'What do we know about media effects on imitation of suicidal behaviour: State of the art.' In D. DeLeo, A. Schmidtke and R. Diekstra (eds) *Suicide Prevention – A Holistic Approach*. Dordrecht: Kluwer.

Schmidtke, A. and Schaller, S. (2000) 'The role of mass media in suicide prevention.' In K. Hawton and K. van Heeringen (eds) *The International Handbook of Suicide and Attempted Suicide*. Chichester: Wiley.

Schotte, D. and Clum, G. (1987) 'Problem-solving skills in suicidal psychiatric patients.' *Journal of Consulting and Clinical Psychology 55*, 49–54.

Sellar, C., Hawton, K. and Goldacre, M. (1990) 'Self-poisoning in adolescents: Hospital admissions and deaths in the Oxford region 1980–85.' *British Journal of Psychiatry 156*, 866–70.

Shaffer, D. (1974) 'Suicide in childhood and early adolescence.' *Journal of Child Psychology and Psychiatry 15*, 275–91.

Shaffer, D. and Craft, L. (1999) 'Methods of adolescent suicide prevention.' *Journal of Clinical Psychiatry 60*, 70–4.

Shaffer, D., Fisher, P., Lucas, C., Dulcan, M. and Schwab-Stone, M. (2000) 'NIMH diagnostic interview schedule for children, version IV (NIMH DISC-IV): Description, differences from previous versions and reliability of some common diagnoses.' *Journal of the American Academy of Child and Adolescent Psychiatry 39*, 28–38.

Shaffer, D., Garland, A., Fisher, P., Bacon, K. and Vieland, V. (1990) 'Suicide crisis centers: A critical reappraisal with special reference to the prevention of youth suicide.' In S. Golston, C. Heinecke and R. Pynoos (eds) *Preventing Mental Health Disturbances in Childhood*. Washington, DC: American Psychiatric Press.

Shaffer, D., Garland, A., Gould, M. and Fisher, P. (1988) 'Preventing teenage suicide: A critical review.' *Journal of the American Academy of Child and Adolescent Psychiatry 27*, 675–87.

Shaffer, D., Gould, M., Fisher, P., Trautman, P., Moreau, D., Kleinman, M. and Flory, M. (1996) 'Psychiatric diagnosis in child and adolescent suicide.' *Archives of General Psychiatry 53*, 339–48.

Shaffer, D. and Piacentini, J. (1994) 'Suicide and attempted suicide.' In M. Rutter, E. Taylor and L. Herzov (eds) *Child and Adolescent Psychiatry: Modern Approaches*. Oxford: Blackwell Scientific.

Shafii, M., Carrigan, S., Wittinghill, J. and Derrick, A. (1985) 'Psychological autopsy of completed suicide in children and adolescents.' *American Journal of Psychiatry 142*, 1061–1064.

Shafii, M. and Shafii, S. (1982) *Pathways to Human Development*. New York: Thieme and Stratton.

Shafii, M., Steltz-Lenarsky, J., Derrick, A., Beckner, C. and Wittinghill, J. (1988) 'Comorbidity of mental disorders in the post-mortem diagnosis of completed suicide in children and adolescents.' *Journal of Affective Disorders 15*, 227–33.

Shneidman, E. (1996) *The Suicidal Mind*. New York: Oxford University Press.

Simonds, J., McMahon, T. and Armstrong, D. (1991) 'Youth suicide attempters compared with a control group: Psychological, affective and attitudinal variables.' *Suicide and Life-Threatening Behaviour 21*, 134–51.

Smith, K. (1990) 'Suicidal behaviour.' *School Psychology Review 19*, 186–95.

Smith, K. and Crawford, S. (1986) 'Suicidal behaviour among "normal" high school students.' *Suicide and Life-Threatening Behaviour 16*, 313–25.

Sonneck, G., Etzersdorfer, E. and Nagel-Kuess, S. (1994) 'Imitative suicide on the Viennese subway.' *Social Science and Medicine 38*, 453–7.

Spandler, H. (1996) *Who's hurting who? Young people, self-harm and Suicide*. Manchester: 42nd Street.

Spirito, A., Brown, L., Overholser, J. and Fritz, G. (1989) 'Attempted suicide in adolescence: A review and critique of the literature.' *Clinical Psychology Review 9*, 335–63.

Spirito, A., Stanton, C., Donaldson, D. and Boergers, J. (2002) 'Treatment-as-usual for adolescent suicide attempters: Implications for the choice of comparison groups in psychotherapy research.' *Journal of Clinical Child and Adolescent Psychology 31*, 41–7.

Spirito, A., Stark, L., Fristad, M., Hart, K. and Owens-Stively, J. (1987) 'Adolescent suicide attempters hospitalised on a paediatric unit.' *Journal of Paediatric Psychology 12*, 171–89.

Spirito, A., Williams, C., Stark, L. and Hart, K. (1988) 'The hopelessness scale for children: Psychometric properties with normal and emotionally disturbed adolescents.' *Journal of Abnormal Child Psychology 16*, 445–58.

Stack, S. (1999) *Media Impacts on Suicide: A Quantitative Review of 293 Findings*. Paper presented at the Annual Meeting of the American Association of Suicidology, Houston, TX.

Steede, K. and Range, L. (1989) 'Does television induce suicidal contagion with adolescents?' *Journal of Community Psychology 17*, 166–72.

Steer, R. and Beck, A. (1988) 'Use of the Beck depression inventory, hopelessness scale, scale for suicidal ideation, and suicidal intent scale with adolescents.' *Advances in Adolescent Mental Health 3*, 219–31.

Steer, R., Kumar, B. and Beck, A. (1993a) 'Hopelessness in adolescent psychiatric inpatients.' *Psychological Reports 72*, 559–64.

Steer, R., Kumar, B. and Beck, A. (1993b) 'Self-reported suicidal ideation in adolescent psychiatric inpatients.' *Journal of Consulting and Clinical Psychology 61*, 1096–9.

Stillion, J. and McDowell, E. (1996) *Suicide Across the Life Span*. Washington DC: Taylor and Francis.

Swedo, S., Rettew, D., Kuppenheimer, M., Lum, D., Dolan, S. and Goldberger, E. (1991) 'Can adolescent suicide attempters be distinguished from at-risk adolescents?' *Paediatrics 88*, 620–9.

Tatman, S., Greene, A. and Karr, L. (1993) 'Use of the suicide probability scale (SPS) with adolescents.' *Suicide and Life-Threatening Behaviour 23*, 188–203.

Taylor, E. and Stansfeld, S. (1984a) 'Children who poison themselves: I. A clinical comparison with psychiatric controls.' *British Journal of Psychiatry 145*, 127–32.

Taylor, E. and Stansfeld, S. (1984b) 'Children who poison themselves: II. Prediction of attendance for treatment.' *British Journal of Psychiatry 145*, 132–5.

Thompson, E. and Eggert, E. (1999) 'Using the suicide risk screen to identify suicidal adolescents among potential high school dropouts.' *Journal of the American Academy of Child and Adolescent Psychiatry 36*, 1506–14.

Tolan, P., Ryan, K. and Jaffe, C. (1988) 'Adolescents' mental health service use and provider process, and recipient characteristics.' *Journal of Clinical Child Psychology 17*, 229–36.

Townsend, E., Hawton, K., Altman, D., Arensman, E., Gunnell, D., Hazell, P., House, A. and Van Heeringen, K. (2001) 'The efficacy of problem-solving treatments after deliberate self-harm: Meta-analysis of randomized controlled trials with respect to depression, hopelessness and improvement in problems.' *Psychological Medicine 31*, 979–88.

Trautman, P., Stewart, N. and Morishima, A. (1993) 'Are adolescent suicide attempters non-compliant with outpatient care?' *Journal of the American Academy of Child and Adolescent Psychiatry 32*, 89–94.

van der Sande, R., Buskens, E., Allart, E., van der Graaf, Y. and van Engeland, H. (1997) 'Psychosocial intervention following suicide attempt: A systematic review of treatment interventions.' *Acta Psychiatrica Scandinavica 96*, 43–50.

Velting, D. and Gould, M. (1977) 'Suicide contagion.' In R. Maris, M. Silberman and S. Canetto (eds) *Review of Suicidology*. New York: Guilford.

Velting, D., Rathus, J. and Asnis, G. (1998) 'Asking adolescents to explain discrepancies in self-reported suicidality.' *Suicide and Life-Threatening Behaviour 28,* 187–96.

Wasserman, I. (1993) 'Comment on hyper media coverage of suicide in New York City.' *Social Science Quarterly 74,* 216–8.

Weissman, M. (1974) 'The epidemiology of suicide attempts.' *Archives of General Psychiatry 30,* 737–46.

Wessely, S., Akhurst, R., Brown, I. and Moss, L. (1996) 'Deliberate self-harm and the probation service: An overlooked public health problem?' *Journal of Public Health Medicine 18,* 129–32.

Wilkinson, G. and Smeeton, N. (1987) 'The repetition of parasuicide in Edinburgh 1980–1981.' *Social Psychiatry 22,* 14–9.

Williams, J. (1997) *Cry of Pain: Understanding Suicide and Self-harm.* Harmondsworth: Penguin.

Williams, J. and Pollock, L. (1993) 'Factors mediating suicidal behaviour: Their utility in primary and secondary prevention.' *Journal of Mental Health 2,* 3–26.

Williams, R. and Morgan, H. (eds) (1994) *Suicide Prevention: The Challenge Confronted. A Manual of Guidance for the Purchasers and Providers of Mental Health Care.* London: NHS Health Advisory Service.

Wilson, A., Passik, S. and Kuras, M. (1989) 'An epigenetic approach to the assessment of personality: The study of instability in stable personality organisations.' In C. Spielberger and J. Butcher (eds) *Advances in Personality Assessment.* Hillsdale, NJ: Erlbaum.

Wilson, W. and Hunter, R. (1983) 'Movie-inspired violence.' *Psychological Reports 53,* 435–41.

World Health Organisation (1992) *The ICD-10 Classification of Mental and Behavioural Disorders: Clinical Descriptions and Diagnostic Guidelines.* Geneva: WHO.

World Health Organisation (1993) *Guidelines for the Primary Prevention of Mental, Neurological and Psychosocial Disorders. 4. Suicide.* Geneva: WHO.

Woznica, J. and Shapiro, J. (1990) 'An analysis of adolescent suicide attempts: The expendable child.' *Journal of Paediatric Psychology 15,* 789–896.

Woznica, J. and Shapiro, J. (1998) 'An analysis of adolescent suicide attempts: A validation of the expendable child measure.' In A. Schwartzberg (ed) *Adolescent in Turmoil.* New York Praeger Publications.

YoungMinds (2003) *Worried About Self-Injury?* London: YoungMinds.

YoungMinds Website: www.youngminds.org.uk.

Zilboorg, B. (1937) 'Considerations on suicide, with particular reference to that of the young.' *American Journal of Orthopsychiatry 7,* 15–31.

Zung, W. (1974) 'Index of potential suicide (IPS): A rating scale for suicide prevention.' In A. Beck, H. Resnik and D. Lettieri (eds) *The Prediction of Suicide.* Bowie, MD: Charles Press Publishers.

Subject Index

Author Index

About Focus

FOCUS was launched in 1997 to promote clinical and organisational effectiveness in child and adolescent mental health services, with an emphasis on incorporating evidence-based research into everyday practice.

Please visit our website to find out more about our work (including our discussion forum and conferences): www.focusproject.org.uk